COPLAS DE YOÇEF
A MEDIEVAL SPANISH POEM
IN HEBREW CHARACTERS

fol. 54v

fol. 56v

MS. 3355, Cambridge University Library

COPLAS DE YOÇEF

A MEDIEVAL SPANISH POEM
IN HEBREW CHARACTERS

Edited with an Introduction and Notes

by

IG. GONZÁLEZ LLUBERA

Professor of Spanish in the Queen's
University of Belfast

The "Coplas de Yoçef" is a fourteenth-century Spanish poem, the manuscript of which is in the University Library, Cambridge. It belongs to that very small class of works in which the words are Spanish, though written in Hebrew characters. In this edition the Hebrew text is printed opposite a transcription into roman character, with an English translation beneath.

CAMBRIDGE
AT THE UNIVERSITY PRESS
1935

CAMBRIDGE
UNIVERSITY PRESS

University Printing House, Cambridge CB2 8BS, United Kingdom

Published in the United States of America by Cambridge University Press, New York

Cambridge University Press is part of the University of Cambridge.

It furthers the University's mission by disseminating knowledge in the pursuit of education, learning and research at the highest international levels of excellence.

www.cambridge.org
Information on this title: www.cambridge.org/9781107421431

First published 1935
First paperback edition 2014

A catalogue record for this publication is available from the British Library

ISBN 978-1-107-42143-1 Paperback

CONTENTS

FRONTISPIECE

Two facsimiles of the MS. *folios 54v, 56v*

FOREWORD

AN EDITION in Latin type of the present text appeared last year in the *Revue Hispanique*, vol. lxxxi (première partie), pages 424–33. This was preceded by a short notice in which a more complete account of the *Coplas*, which would include the text in Hebrew characters, was stated to be in preparation. I publish now the transcription in Hebrew type accompanied by the edition in Latin type and an English translation. Palaeographical notes have been provided, and the philological commentary has been enlarged. In a final section of parallels and sources the *Sepher ha-Yashar* and Old Spanish biblical versions have been quoted at length. The English version of the quotations from the *Yashar* is based on the New York edition (1840). This however has been revised and altered in accordance with the Warsaw Hebrew edition (1927). It is hoped in this way that the book may be useful both to Hispanists and students of Jewish literature.

The philological value of the text is somewhat diminished by the almost entire absence of vowel-points in the MS. In the circumstances my interpretation in so far as the vowels is concerned is necessarily conjectural. In the transcription of the consonants I have adhered to the system followed in the *Revue Hispanique*. But it has seemed convenient to adopt the symbol ǧ for ‍ג. Moreover, the present edition differs from the previous one in several points of textual interpretation (comp. lines 79, 108, 134 among others). In the transcription in Hebrew characters no emendations have been introduced, the square brackets merely denoting blurred or doubtful letters or signs in the MS. But the text has been printed in verse form, so as to include two haxasyllables in a line. In the edition in Latin type the text, besides being vocalised, has been emended whenever it has been deemed necessary. All additions and alterations are indicated by square brackets, and suggested suppressions by parentheses. The rejected readings are recorded in the footnotes.

It is a pleasure to acknowledge my indebtedness to Mr Herbert Loewe, Reader in Rabbinic Literature in the University of Cambridge, who first brought to my notice the existence of the MS. I am deeply grateful to him for his generous assistance and continued interest in the progress of my work. I desire further to record my thanks to the editor of the *Revue Hispanique* for her consent to incorporate the text and some of the footnotes from my previous edition; to the officers of the Cambridge University Library, in particular to Dr E. J. Thomas, for providing me with photographs of the MS.; to Dr J. Leveen, of the Oriental Department of the British Museum; to Dr Pere Bohigas, of the University of Barcelona; and to Mr M. Welland, B.A., for his revision of the English rendering of the text. Finally, I must mark my sense of great obligation to the Syndics of the Cambridge University Press for sponsoring the publication of the book.

IG. G. LL.

BELFAST
January 1935

ABBREVIATIONS

Alex*O* = *El Libro de Alexandre*. BAE, vol. 57.

Alex*P* = *El Libro de Alixandre*. Manuscrit esp. 488 de la Bibliothèque Nationale de Paris, publié par A. Morel-Fatio. Dresden 1906.

Apol = *Libro de Apolonio*. Ed. C. C. Marden. I. Text and introduction. II. Grammar, notes and vocabulary. Princeton-Paris 1917–21.

BAE = Biblioteca de Autores Españoles.

BAlba = Biblia traducida del hebreo al castellano por Rabí Mosé Arragel de Guadalfajara (1422–33?). Tomo I. [Madrid] 1920.

BEsc = Biblia medieval romanceada. Según los MSS. Escurialenses I-j-3, I-j-8, I-j-6. Vol. I. Pentateuco. Ed. A. Castro, A. Millares Carlo, A. J. Battistessa. Buenos Aires 1927.

BFerrar = *Biblia en lengua española*. Ferrara 5313 [1553].

BProv = *Libro de los Buenos Proverbios*. Ed. Knust.

DL = R. Menéndez-Pidal, Documentos Lingüísticos de España. I. Reino de Castilla. Madrid 1919.

Duran = Documents aljamiats de jueus catalans. Extret del "Butlletí de la Biblioteca de Catalunya", vol. v. Barcelona 1920

Esther = Le roman provençal d'Esther, par Crescas du Caylar, médecin juif du xive siècle. Ed. Neubauer-P. Meyer (Ro xxi, pp. 194 ff.).

FGz = *Poema de Fernan Gonzalez*. Ed. C. C. Marden. Baltimore 1904.

Gassner = Das altspanische Verbum. Halle 1897.

GEst = Alfonso el Sabio, *General Estoria*. Primera parte. Ed. A. G. Solalinde. Madrid 1930.

Grünbaum = Jüdisch-Spanische Chrestomathie. Frankfurt a.M. 1896.

Hanssen = Gramática Histórica de la Lengua Castellana. Halle 1913.

JRuiz = *Libro de Buen Amor*. Ed. Ducamin. Toulouse 1901.

Knust = Mittheilungen aus dem Eskurial. Tübingen 1879.

MCid = *Poema de Mio Cid*. Ed. M. Pidal (*Cantar* III).

Milagr = Berceo, *Milagros de Nuestra Señora*. Ed. A. G. Solalinde. Madrid 1922.

Millàs = Documents hebraics de jueus catalans. Barcelona 1927.

MPidal *Cantar* = Cantar de Mio Cid. Texto Gramática y Vocabulario. Madrid 1908–11.

—— *Or* = Orígenes del español. Madrid 1926.

MPolo = *El Libro de Marco Polo.* Ed. Knust-Stuebe. Leipzig 1902.

PCG = *Primera Crónica General.* Ed. M. Pidal. Madrid 1906.

PConst = חמשי חומשי תורה...תרגום המקרא בלשון יון ולשון לעז [Pentateuch, with Greek and Spanish translation in Hebrew script.] Constantinople 1547.

RAlex = *El rrekontamiento del rrey Ališandre.* Ed. A. R. Nykl (RHi vol. 77).

RArch = Revista de Archivos. Madrid.

RFE = Revista de Filología Española. Madrid.

RHi = Revue Hispanique. New York-Paris.

Ro = Romania. Paris.

SDom = Berceo, *Vida de Santo Domingo de Silos.* Ed. J. D. FitzGerald. Paris 1904.

SGFr = Spanish Grail Fragments. Ed. Pietsch. I. Texts. II. Commentary. Chicago 1924–5.

Shem Tob*C* = [*Proverbios Morales*]. MS. Cantabr. Add. 3355, fols. 1–53.

—— *E* = Los versos del rabi don Santo. MS. Escur. iv, 6, 21, fols. 1–86.

—— *M* = El libro del rab don Santob. MS. Bca. Nac. Madrid, Bb-82, fols. 61–81.

Staaff = Étude sur le dialecte Léonais. Uppsala 1907.

VTristan = *El cuento de Tristan de Leonis.* Ed. from the MS. Vatican 6428, by G. T. Northup. Chicago 1928.

Wagenaar = La négation en ancien espagnol. Groningen 1931.

Yashar = ס״הישר. Warsaw 5688 [1927].

Yuçuf*A* — *Poema de Yuçuf* (MS. Acad. Hist.). Ed. Menéndez Pidal (RArch vi).

—— *B* = Poema de Yuçuf (MS. Bca. Nac.). Ed. Morf. Leipzig 1883.

ZRPh = Zeitschrift für romanische Philologie.

INTRODUCTION

I

T H E story of Joseph has been the subject of various paraphrases in prose and verse in the medieval vernaculars, apart from biblical translations.[1] In Spanish literature it occupies sixty chapters of the *General Estoria*,[2] appears under a Moorish garb in the *Poema de Yuçuf*[3] and later "legends of Joseph",[4] and inspires among others two important plays in the sixteenth and early seventeenth century theatre.[5]

The fragments now edited bring to our notice the existence of a hitherto unknown Jewish "Yuçuf". But the parallel between the

[1] For Latin versions, see Manitius, *Gesch. der latein. Lit. des Mittelalters*, I, 568. In view of the time of its composition and of its author's nationality, the *Historia Joseph translata de arabico in latinum per fratrem Alfonsum Bonihominis Hispanum ordinis predicatorum* (1336) is of particular interest. This work remains unpublished to my knowledge (see Mussafia's notice in *Sitzungsber. k. Akad. d. Wissensch. zu Wien, phil.-hist. Klasse*, xlviii, 265). The *Estoire de Joseph*, which dates from the later part of the twelfth century (see ed. Steuer, Erlangen 1902, p. 29), is one of the earliest vernacular renderings, whilst the ME "Iacob and Ioseph" belongs to the second half of the thirteenth century (ed. Napier, Oxford 1916). A MHG verse paraphrase was edited by J. Diemer in the Vienna *Sitzungsber*. xlvii, 636; xlviii, 339. The Catalan paraphrase by Joan Roiç de Corella is a good specimen of "valenciana prosa" (ed. Miquel i Planas, Barcelona 1913).

[2] Lib. viii, caps. 5–13, 16–26; ix, 1–15, 17–39, 43–7 (ed. Solalinde, vol. i, pp. 208–63).

[3] Of uncertain date. Two MSS., one from the fourteenth, the other from the sixteenth century. The latter has been edited several times, among other scholars by H. Morf (Leipzig 1883); the former by Menéndez Pidal (RArch vi, 91, 276, 347).

[4] MSS. at the Bca. Nac. Madrid. Transcription by F. Guillén Robles, *Leyendas de José, hijo de Jacob* (Bibl. Aut. Aragoneses, v), Zaragoza 1888.

[5] For the history of the subject in sixteenth-century Spanish theatre, see Cañete, *Teatro español del siglo xvi*, pp. 107–212, and J. E. Gillet's introduction to his edition of the *Comedia Josefina* by Micael de Carvajal (Elliott Monographs, xxviii, Princeton Univ. Press 1932). On Lope de Vega's *Los Trabajos de Jacob*, see Menéndez Pelayo, *Estudios sobre el teatro de L. de V.* vol. i, pp. 164–75.

Morisco and the Jewish works extends to aspects other than the identity of their main subject, and in this respect it is regrettable that the account of those episodes which would include in all probability important parallels to the former poem are missing in our MS. Both poems appear to have been written in the respective national scripts. Thus the MS. with which the present essay is concerned forms a valuable addition to the meagre amount of Hebrew *aljamiado* materials accessible to us, whilst within the field of Jewish Spanish literature generally it contains an important portion of the earliest poetical rendering so far known of that biblical story.[1]

II

The MS. Add. 3355 in the Cambridge University Library[2] contains a defective copy of the *Proverbios Morales* by Shem Tob de Carrión, besides the fragments of the *Yoçef* now published. It is a paper codex of 61 leaves, 10 × 8 cm., written in single columns, as prose, 14 lines to the page as a rule. Some have 13 and a few 15 lines. The writing is by one hand throughout. In folios 54, 60 and 60 *v*, scribblings in a rough and thick hand appear in the margin or in the blanks between portions of the text. The codex is unbound and imperfect at the beginning and at the end. The edges of the leaves are very worn. They have been recently numbered in pencil and are distributed into five quires.

The first quire (fols. 1–15 in the order of the present foliation) has 15 leaves. Fol. 15 is detached, but the catchword איל on the lower margin of the verso side corresponds with the beginning of the next page, thus showing that the first leaf of the quire is missing.

The second quire has 16 leaves (fols. 16–31). The catchword איל on fol. 31 *v* fits in with the beginning of the following page.

The third quire is also of 16 leaves (fols. 32–47), but the catchword איש on fol. 47 *v* does not correspond with the initial word of fol. 48.

The fourth quire contains 6 leaves only (fols. 48–53). In view of the

---

[1] Later Jewish Spanish versions include the following: *Comedia de la vida y sucesos de Joseph* by Iṣḥaq Matitia Aboab, which has remained unpublished in a MS. from Amsterdam, dated 5446 (1686), according to *Notice de la bibliothèque de S. Sarphati* (Amsterdam 1866), no. 1881; *Coplas de Yoseph ha-Ṣaddiq* by Abraham de Toledo, Constantinople 1732; *Conplas de Yoçef*, in *Roscas de Purim*, Vienna 1866 (Grünbaum, p. 143).

[2] It was acquired by this library in 1896, from Jerusalem, as Dr E. J. Thomas kindly informs me. But I have been unable to establish the previous whereabouts of the MS.

xii

composition of the preceding quires, we can assume the loss of 10 leaves in the present one. The context shows, on the other hand, that it is incomplete both at the beginning and at the end.

The fifth quire has 8 leaves (fols. 54–61). It is also incomplete at the beginning and at the end. A careful inspection of the codex proves that this quire preceded the other four in the original arrangement.[1] This is shown by the direction of the binding strings, and is corroborated by the comparatively dilapidated state of fols. 53v and 54, where the text is more blurred than in the rest of the MS., particularly on fol. 54r, where several words have become illegible. Both leaves must have been left unprotected for a long period of time.

From the data given below it may safely be inferred that three quires have been lost at the beginning of the MS. It seems reasonable to suppose that the present fifth quire and those that preceded it were of 16 leaves, and that 4 leaves at the beginning and 4 at the end of that quire are now missing.

We may conclude that in the complete MS. the *Coplas de Yoçef* preceded the *Proverbios Morales*, and that the former work filled over 61 leaves. As to the latter, over four-fifths of the total number of stanzas in the Madrid MS. are extant in the present copy (fols. 1–53).[2] The fragments now edited comprise therefore the 8 extant leaves of the fifth quire (fols. 54–61, according to the present foliation).

The water-mark proves that the MS. probably belongs to the first half of the fifteenth century. The mark—a cart with two wheels—belongs to the period between 1413 and 1473. Mr Herbert Loewe, to whom I am indebted on this point, is inclined to date the make of the paper between 1430 and 1450.[3]

The fortunate circumstance that the scribe frequently states the

[1] In the preface to the edition which appeared in the RHi, lxxxi (1ère partie), 421, it was stated that a quire must be missing between the present fourth and fifth quires. I was not aware of the original arrangement of the MS. at that time.

[2] Namely 560 stanzas. A detailed account of the state of the text will appear in my edition of the *Proverbios*.

[3] See Briquet, I, p. 229. Our mark—which occurs in fols. 11, 14, 26, 27, 34, 49—partly coincides with that of the Perpignan makes of 1412, 1432 (Briquet, no. 3527), partly with those of Barcelona, Montpellier, Perpignan, of 1429–61 (ibid. no. 3528). On the other hand the frame marks are alike throughout the MS. There is little doubt that all the paper in the codex is of one kind.

number of the stanzas allows us to calculate the approximate extent of the work. Two stanzas on fol. 54*v* are numbered 265, 266. The first stanza on fol. 54*r*—no break in the narrative being discernible in the immediately preceding ones—must be the 261st. The average number of stanzas per leaf being five, the 260 preceding stanzas must have filled 52 leaves, i.e. three quires of 16 leaves, and 4 leaves. Thus the present defective quire, when complete, would begin at stanza 241.

The context shows that a few stanzas at the most are missing at the end. The poem would thus end on the missing leaf following the present 61, bringing the total number of stanzas up to the 312 or thereabout.

The present text is a copy from an already defective MS. In two places (fols. 60 and 60*v*) the scribe has left a four-line blank, and in each case it is stated that a stanza is missing. Such omissions point to a dilapidated copy having existed from which the present one was made. That the copy was not only in a bad state of preservation, but was defective as well, is apparent from the fact that after l. 28 no indication is forthcoming from the scribe with regard to those stanzas that both the sequence of the narrative and the numbering show to be missing at that spot.[1]

In conclusion, the present copy must be removed by at least two stages from the original version. Moreover, there is abundant proof of the corrupt state of the text: distorted lines (54–5), dittographies (e.g. l. 119), identical rime-words (146–7), and ll. 35, 46, 79, 108, 135, etc. show errors of transcription of one kind or another.

III

The handwriting of the MS. belongs to a cursive Spanish variety, of which examples are abundant from the later part of the thirteenth to the end of the sixteenth centuries. Our scribe's hand is not dissimilar to that of the British Museum MS. Sloane, 3029.[2] The main features of that hand are as follows:

1. Two types of א are used: (*a*) The standard one, as in מאנו (54*v*,l. 3), ויאיאה (56*v*,l. 1). (*b*) A more cursive one, as in אאיבמו (ibid.l. 6),[3] which

---

[1] See note *in loc.*

[2] Margoliouth, *Catal. Hebr. and Samar. MSS.* III, pl. 11.

[3] A similar type of א is regularly used in a Barcelona charter of 1274 (Millàs, facs. 33); in the specimen from the fifteenth-century book of accounts of the Daroca synagogue (*Manuscr. árabes y aljamiados de la bca. de la Junta*, Madrid 1912, facs. 18, passim); and in the *Ordinació de la Claveria del call de Cervera* (1445), in Duran, pp. 9–14.

is sometimes practically indistinguishable from one of the varieties of נ
in the MS. as in the second of איאיל, l. 99. In the ligature א (54*v*, l. 2)
the א is notably deformed.

2. ג is of the usual cursive shape. It consists of two strokes of about
the same length, one vertical, the other horizontal. They meet at a right
angle towards the lower left end of the vertical stroke. The length and
position of the horizontal stroke result in the following letter being
written within the ג, as a rule, e.g. the א of גֿאקוב (54*v*, l. 6); or the
second ו of לואיגן (ibid.), etc.

3. The angular upper turning of the ד clearly differentiates this letter
from the ר. The marked oblique falling from right to left of the vertical
stroke, as in ויידן (54*v*, l. 12), is characteristic of this script.

4. Besides the current type, ה adopts sometimes a shape not unlike
Ar. ﻫ. This is caused by the linking of that letter with a preceding א,
ב, ם, as in טיניאה (56*v*, l. 4).

5. ו may be linked to the lower left end of a preceding ב: ביבֿו
(54*v*, l. 8).

6. י may be reduced to a mere dot. In several instances this dot
appears to be duplicated without any phonetic consequences, that is,
the two stand for one letter. They may be placed so close together as to
become almost indistinguishable from each other, as in the second י
of ריסיביר (54*v*, l. 2).[1] Whenever two יי are meant, they are always
separately written, and their shape is sufficiently stressed so as to make
confusion impossible: comp. פידיירה (54*v*, l. 3), דיין (56*v*, l. 7). When
preceded by a ב, ד, or ר, the י, יי are written within these letters:
שביאה (54*v*, l. 8), דישקי (ibid. l. 1).

7. The two varieties of מ used in the MS. are exemplified by מוי
(54*v*, l. 1) and מי (56*v*, last line). Final ם is rounded like a ם in square
script: קום (56*v*, l. 11).[2]

8. The main varieties of נ used by our scribe may be studied in
נונקה (54*v*, l. 8), ויניֿרה (ibid. l. 13), גֿינטי (56*v*, l. 1).

---

[1] That in such cases a single letter is meant becomes clear when we ob-
serve that so as to avoid confusion the two dots are joined by a stroke,
whenever they are placed too far apart.

[2] This type of ם is also current in the charters published by Millàs, and
Duran i Sampere.

9. The upper turning of ר is nearly always clearly rounded. On one or two occasions, however, the falling stroke is identical with that of a ד. This occurs in the ר of פֿראבֿה, l. 79.

10. שׁ assumes the shape of an initial נ followed by ט. The only appreciable difference lies in the upper left stroke, which is roughly semicircular in the case of the ט, but flatter in the שׁ: comp. שׁ in אִישׁ (56v, l. 7), and נט in גִּינטִי (ibid. l. 8).

11. The various forms of ת are exemplified in אומילדֿאת and וירדֿאת (54v, ll. 10–11).

12. The diacritic mark over בֿ, גֿ, פֿ and שׂ is as a rule a dot. In a few instances, however, it appears as an acute accent: לִיֿוֹראבָֿאן, l. 86; מוֹגֿוֹ, l. 126; or as two strokes, either parallel to one another, or in the shape of an inverted circumflex accent, as in פֿוֹאירטִי, l. 29; פָֿאיִשׁ, l. 68. On final ף a stroke is always used. It does not possess, however, any diacritic significance.[1] It seems to be a cursive survival of the flourish that the upper ending of both ף and פ present in certain Spanish MSS. The mark over שׂ, denoting Sp *x*, is always placed on the left of that letter, and its position is not altered in our transcription.

The following signs are used to indicate the beginning and end of lines or stanzas: (*a*) A line of three or more dots (⸵) close to the initial letter of a word indicates the beginning of a stanza. (*b*) Three dots arranged in a triangle at the end of a word denote the conclusion of a stanza. (*c*) A single dot marks the end of a line.

IV

Romance orthographical symbols are represented in the MS. in accordance with the following principles:

1. In initial position, א stands for *a*, whenever it is not followed by ו or י. This vowel is always expressed at the beginning, and often in the middle of a word: גֿוֹראבה *ǧurabaʰ* 72, פֿראבֿה *paravaʰ* 79; but

[1] Apart from the proper noun יוֹסף, it appears in the word פרינסיף (Shem Tob*C* fol. 18, last line), which cannot be transcribed other than as *prinçep*. As to the former, the spelling shows that the Hebrew pronunciation was intended. It seems clear that with a Hebrew word there is no need for a diacritic representing a Spanish sound.

אירמגוש *erm[a]nos* 25. Its use in pretonic or posttonic position is less regular: פֿאיינדו *faziendo* 79, אטאבוד *atabud* 84, פּראבאן *paravan* 99, אמאבאן *amavan* 88; but פדרי *p[a]dre* 14, מנירה *m[a]nera*[h] 22, פינשארן *pensar[a]n* 139. At the end of a word, א stands either alone, as in אייא *aya* 71, אלייא *alya* 67, יא *ya* 80, לא *la* 29; or followed by a ה: דיזיאה *dezia*[h] 17. In אה *a*[h], the ה is never omitted, except when joined with the following word, as in איוסף *a Yoçef* 116. As a rule, however, final *a* is not expressed, and its presence is indicated by ה: מנירה *maner[a]*[h] 17, and passim. א is also used as a graphic device to denote the vocalic pronunciation of a ו or י immediately following. In this connexion it always appears in words which begin with *i-, e-, o-, u-*: אי *i* 53, אירמגוש *ermanos* 24, אוטראש *otras* 98, אושאבאן *usaban* 52. A similar function is fulfilled by א in the middle of a word, when ו and י, or א and ו, both representing vowels, occur, either in hiatus, or forming a diphthong. In such words א is written between the two letters: לואיגו *luego* 17, אאון *aun* 18; but מוי *mu-i* 13, *mui* 16. Finally, when *ei* is meant, א is placed between the two יי: ריאי *re-i* 22, ויאיאה *ve-i-a*[h] 57, ריאיש *reis* 26.

2. ב = Sp *b*: בואינוש *buenos* 102, שבידיש *sabedes* 117. A diacritic mark on the ב denotes the consonantic value of OSp *v, u*: סיבירה *çivera*[h] 55, קאבבה *kavava*[h] 125. The omission of the mark when ב stands for the fricative is not rare. In several instances it is probably due to the scribe's carelessness, as in פבלאבה *fablaba*[h] 126, אובו *obo* 109, etc. Other examples, however, point to confusion of the sounds *b* and *v*, and consequent orthographic vacillation.[1] It should be noticed that although Sp *v* is also rendered by ו, ב is more generally employed. This is always the case with the desinential -*v*- of the imperfect in the verbs in -*ar*.

3. ג = Sp postpalatal *g*: גישאבאן *gisavan* 97, מגירה *magera*[h] 60. OSp *j*, also the affricate *ch*, are rendered by ג with a diacritic mark: גינטיש *ǧentes* 49, מוגאש *muǧas* 98. Thus an early Romance spelling

---

[1] In about one-fourth of the total number of words in which fric. *v* has been rendered by ב the diacritic point has been omitted. (Comp. RArch vi, p. 114.)

of both the fricative *ž* and the affricate *č* by *g* is perpetuated in Hebrew transliteration.[1]

4. ד = *d*: דִישׁוֹ *dixo* 45, אִישטִידוּ *estido* 61, אטאבוד *atabud* 71. It is impossible to say if the dot which appears over this letter on three occasions (מִירסִיד *merçed* 68, מאנדֿאמיינטו *mandamiento* 81, קונגֿוראדו *konǧurado* 90) has been intentionally used by the scribe.

5. With the single exception of הורן *horo* 7, ה is only used as a final letter. In this word it stands for Sp *h*.[2] At the end of a word its use in *aljamiado* is merely a survival of Hebrew orthography in words ending in ָה, in which the consonant is a mere orthographic indication of the preceding vowel. In consequence, when at the end of a word in -*a*, it possesses no phonetic value in Hebrew transcription of Spanish sounds. This is corroborated in our MS. by those words in which final *a* is indifferently transcribed by א- or אה-.

6. ו stands: (*a*) For the vowels *o*, *u*: שׁורדו *sordo* 125, גֿורה *ǧurah* 69, אושׁאבאן *usaban* 52, אוטראשׁ *otras* 98; and for *u* in the diphthong *ue*: פֿואירטי *fuerte* 29. (*b*) For the consonant *v*: אויאה *aviah* 63, סיורה *çiverah* 44, ואניײאר *vanyar* 82.[3]

7. ז = OSp *z*: דיזיאה *deziah* 17, דיז *diez* 159.

8. In Spanish words ח only occurs in חורושׁ *ḥoros* 166 (comp. *horo* 7).[4]

9. Sp *t*, in initial and medial position, is rendered by ט: טייראשׁ *tieras* 49, גֿינטישׁ *ǧentes* 49.

10. י is used: (*a*) For the vowels *i*, *e*, in which case it fulfils a similar function to that of Hebr. י, when a *ḥireq* or a *ṣere* is assumed in the preceding consonant: דִישׁירה *dixerah* 65, מִירסִיד *merçed* 68.[5] The diphthong *ie* is rendered by יי, whilst יא stands for *ei* (as noticed before); יא—אה at the end of a word—renders -*ia*; and יו, -*io*: טיירה *tierah* 29, ריא *re-i* 22, ריאישׁ *reis* 26, דיאה *diah* 138, אוסיאראן *oçiaran* 133,

---

[1] The adoption of one symbol for both sounds may be taken to imply an affricate pronunciation of OSp *j* (see MPidal *Or* § 8, 1–3). In JCatalan a similar symbol stands for both *ž* and *š* (Duran p. 7).

[2] The name יהודה is not taken into account.

[3] In עשׁו, ו is rendered by *w* in the present transcription.

[4] יצחק has not been taken into account.

[5] The vowel *e* is not always indicated, although such cases as אינטראר *ent[e]rar* 70 (comp. 94) must be ascribed to the copyist.

דין *Dio* 58. Clear cases of two יי representing a single vowel sound do not seem to occur in this part of the MS.[1] (*b*) The consonant *y* is rendered by one, less often by two יי: יא *ya* 152, יאזן *yazen* 70, יאזיי *yazie* 161, אייא *aya* 71.[2]

11. ל = *l*: לה *la^h* 15, סיילוש *çielos* 69. The symbol *ll* is represented by ל followed by one or two יי, constantly one, if the palatal precedes a ו: לייאמו *lyamar* 64 (comp. ליאמאר Shem Tob*C* fol. 14, 1. 17), קונטראליאדור *kontralyador* 106.[3] In פוליאה *folia^h* 139, we have the perpetuation of the Romance spelling of the palatal by a single *l*; but לינארון 141 may be due to an oversight, as *lle*- is usually rendered by ליי (comp. לייגאדו *lyegado* Shem Tob*C* fol. 4, 1. 3).

12. מ, ם = *m*: מישורה *mesura^h* 96, קום *kom* 3.

13. נ, ן = *n*: נון *non* 127, וינדיזיאה *vendezia^h* 75. Palatal *ñ* is rendered by ני or ניי, thus reproducing the spelling *ny*: אניוש *anyos* 159, ואניאר *vanyar* 82.[4]

14. ס = OSp *ç*: סיילוש *çielos* 69, אובידיסיירון *obedeçieron* 102.[5]

15. In the Hebrew name עשו *'Esaw* (109, and passim), only, the letter ע appears.

16. פ = *p*: פלאזיר *plazer* 20. With a diacritic it stands for *f*: פֿואירו *fuero* 52. Final ף occurs in the name יוסף *Yoçef*, where it stands for Hebr. *f*.[6] The diacritic is not clear in פֿושורה *fosura^h* 71, פֿינאדו *finado* 91. It has doubtless been omitted in דיפינדיר *de-[f]ender* 6.

[1] See III, § 6. Two יי with the value of *e* occur in the Provençal Esther: גיינולש *genols* 24, גיינטא *genta* 34, etc.

[2] The spelling of *i* as first element of a diphthong, and consonantic *y* by יי, seems more general in PConst. Thus *dio* is rendered דייו in that work. In modern JSp orthography *i* in the diphthongs *ai, oi, ui, ia, io, iu*, is generally expressed by יי (see RHi i, 25). Comp. קובדיסייא *kobdiçia* Shem Tob*C* fol. 23, קאמייו *kamio* ibid. fol. 31*v*.

[3] The spelling לי for *ll* perpetuates *ly* of Romance orthography (see MPidal *Or* § 5, 9). It also occurs in JCatalan (Duran p. 7), and in Esther it renders Prov. *lh*. In modern JSp ליי (= *y*) is general.

[4] See MPidal *Or* § 4, 1. I find the same spelling in the transcription of a Catalan name in a thirteenth-century Hebrew charter (Millàs, facs. 28, 1).

[5] Also in JCatalan (Duran p. 13, 6).

[6] Had the scribe intended to reproduce a Romance spelling he would have written יוסׅף.

17. צ occurs in יצחק *Yiṣḥaq* 114, 115. In the transcription of Romance words it is not used except in one instance, ראיץ *raiç*, (Shem Tob*C* fol. 53), where it stands for OSp *ç*.

18. ק = *k*, namely the postpalatal stop: קונשיגֿו *konseǧo* 25. In the Hebrew name יצחק I transcribe it by *q*.[1]

19. ר represents both single *r* and trilled *r*, *rr*: ראזון *razon* 9, טיירה *tier[r]a^h* 29, פֿואירה *fuera^h* 56.[2] As this spelling also prevails in the transcription of Romance languages other than Spanish into Hebrew script, its adoption is merely a persistence of Hebrew orthographic usage.

20. שׂ = OSp *ss*, *s*. No special device is adopted by the scribe to differentiate the voiced and voiceless sounds: בישׁאבה *besava^h* 80, פושׁיירון *pusieron* 103, שׁושׁיגׁאבה *sosegava^h* 155, פֿשׁאשׁין *pasasen* 108. The addition of a diacritic mark on שׁ gives this letter the value of OSp *x*: דישׁו *dixo* 45.[3]

21. ת is used only at the end of a word,[4] and represents the sound which OSp orthography transcribes by *th*, *t*, *d*: בונדראת *bondath* 119.[5]

22. The MS. is, as a rule, unpointed. The use of the vowel-points seems restricted to certain cases when confusion might arise, as in וְי טוּ *ve tu* 122, אַקֵי *ake* 150, or else to stress the pronunciation of certain vowels: וִישׁטוּ *vistu* 18.[6] Š*e*wa has no phonetic significance. In view of the punctuation פִֿיזְיירה *fizyera^h* 105, שׁוֹנְשַׁאנְיוֹשׁ *sonsanyos* 157, it may be surmised that the scribe had in mind an orthographic *y*, as the equivalent of a following י in Romance orthography.[7]

---

[1] ק is very often adopted for κ in the Talmudic transcription of Greek words (see Strack-Siegfried, *Lehrb. neuhebr. Spr.* § 5). כ does not occur in our MS. excepting the Hebrew word כאן (Shem Tob*C* fol. 50*v*).

[2] Comp. MPidal *Or* p. 83. It is a well-known spelling in later orthography: *acorer* Alex*P* 176d, *desterado* Apol 130a, *caçura* JRuiz 114a, *deramo* VTristan, intr. p. 5, etc.

[3] The diacritic mark always appears on the left of the שׂ, and I transcribe it accordingly.

[4] Hebr. נפתלי *Naftali* 121, is not taken into account.

[5] See MPidal *Cantar* II, § 85.

[6] The vowel-points are in the same hand as the rest of the MS.

[7] Š*e*wa appears to be used here as in PConst. See also the JFrench poems edited by Blondheim (*Poèmes Judéo-Français*, Paris 1927, pp. 50 ff.).

23. In accordance with prevalent usage in Romance orthography, certain prepositions are often written together with the following definite article, and also with certain pronouns and even nouns. Thus אלה *ala^h* 23, אלאש *alas* 49; אטי *ati* 31, אווש *avos* 119, אאיל *ael* 86, אאיליוש *aelyos* 56, אשו *asu* 14; אטודוש *atodos* 156; איוסף *a Yoçef* 11 (but *a^h Yoçef* 12, etc.; *a^h Ğakob* 100, etc.); דילה *dela^h* 47, קוניל *konel* 7, איניל *enel* 87, אינישי *enese* 138. Adherence to the prevailing usage is also shown in the spelling of adverbs of manner: סיירטה מינטי *çierta^h mente* 31, אפרישוראדה מינטי *apresurada^h mente* 32; also the pronouns ווש אוטרוש *vos otros* 117, and קון ווישקו *kon vusko* 168 (comp. *kon nusko* Shem Tob C fol. 42 v).

The preceding analysis corroborates the adherence of Hispano-Hebraic transliteration to archaic Romance spellings (*ny, ly, mr*), which may be an indication of origin, inasmuch as such spellings lingered in dialectal regions, where the standard symbols *ll, nn, nbr* were not universally adopted till later. Taken as a whole, the orthography, as shown in the adoption of diacritic marks and also in the little use made of duplicated consonants functioning as a single Romance symbol, is more accurate and systematic than that of Caslari's Esther in Provençal.

V

The omission of the vowel-points in the MS. deprives us of some important data in the linguistic study of the text: we are unable to determine the nature of certain vowels, as the orthography is apt to represent by י both *e* and *i*, by ו, *o* and *u*. In such cases our interpretation is bound to be conjectural. On the other hand the comparative shortness of the present fragments precludes a comprehensive grammatical account. The following linguistic features, however, may be recorded:

(A) 1. Monophthongization of secondary *au* occurs in *oçiar* 133.

2. Absorption of the first element of the diphthong *ie* by a preceding palatal is apparent in *koğentes* 51, *dekoğeron* 104.

3. The pointing of the scribe shows modification of the pretonic vowel in *fizyera^h* 105, *komidyera^h* 131.

4. Final ו is pointed וּ = *u* in *ditu* 6, *maderu* 10, *vistu* 18.

5. Judging by the metre, hiatus occurs in *re-i* in 22, 92; *re-is* 104 (possibly also in 101); *mu-i* 13, 16, 21, 81, 156. Synaeresis must be

xxi

effected in *reis* 26, *rei* 89; *mui* 75, 78, 143. Hiatus is confirmed by the metre or may be surmised in *se-er* 99, *se-ertemos* 146, *a-un* 18, 60; *pri-ado* 81, 125; *enbi-ava*[h] 11; *o-inavan* 100, *A-ibto* 5 and passim. Synaeresis is constant in the imperfect *-ie* (53, 37, 41, 139, 161); and also in *fue* 82, *Dio* 69, 58, 93; *vendiçion* 76.

6. Apocope of *-o* is shown in *kom* 3, 147 (but *komo* 23, 37, 84, 102);[1] of *-e* in *sabte* 130.[2] Loss of *e* also occurs: (*a*) With the preposition *de* in combination with pronouns having initial *e*: *del* 142, *dese* 6, *desta*[h] 22, 89, 109; *di*, if our interpretation is correct (see note to 8). (*b*) With *delante* + pron. *el*, and *entre* + *ellos*: 50, 71. (*c*) With the pronouns *me*, *te*, when proclitic to forms of the verb *aver* in the future tense: *sakarte* 7, *dezirte* 65, *levarmas* 67, *seertemos* 146. In the following words apocope is necessary: *grand(e)* 58, *levas(e)* 91, *tod(o)* 105 (but *todo* 42, 44), *testament(o)* 160, *kuand(o)* 149. See also *dizien* (note to 145). Enclitic forms of *me*, *le*, *se*, *te* are required by the metre in the following passages: *e t(e)* 6, *alya m(e)* 67, *ke l(e)* 91, *trayem(e)* 123, *muerto s(e)* 129. Aphaeresis may be suspected, on the same basis, in *do (e)stavan* 94, *aki (e)stava*[h] 127 (comp. Apol. II, p. 8). There is a case of epenthetic *-e-* in *salderedes* (see note to 167).

7. Fricative pronunciation of initial *b* (after a vowel or *s*) is shown by the spellings *vendezia*[h] 75, *vendiçion* 76, *vanyar* 82. The usual dissimilation of *b-* in *bivir* occurs in *bivos* 167. In *bibiera*[h] 159, the diacritic point on the second *b* has been carelessly omitted by the scribe.

8. Initial *h-* appears once only (*horo* 7, which is transcribed with ה in 166).[3] Etymological *f-* is always retained. The demonstrative *he* is rendered without any sign of aspiration.[4]

9. Intervocalic *b* is used in numerous instances as a fricative, instead of *v*. Thus against *çivera*[h] 44, 45, we have *çibera*[h]; against *avemos* 43, *ove* 110, *ovo* 15, 89, there is *abie* 53, *obo* 109, *abredes* 151; the desinential *-ava*[h] (thus usually spelt) becomes *-aba*[h] in 77, 126; *servientes* 97, 146 alternates with *serbientes* 50. *kueba*[h] only appears with *b*. The etymological intervocalic is kept in *atabud* 71, and the weakness of the fricative is shown in *priado* 81, 125, as against *privado* 13. Disappearance of *-g-* gives rise to the characteristic form *Aibto*.[5]

---

[1] See 3, note.
[2] Also *diz* 69, 165.
[3] The orthography of PConst betrays a similar hesitation: הָארִי *hare*, חאראש *ḥaras* (fols. 92 a, 22, 28, etc.).
[4] See 146, note.
[5] See 5, note.

10. There is no trace of dialectal treatment of the groups *pl, cl, ct, l't, c'l,* etc. that I can detect. Thus *lyamar* 73, *lyanto* 87, *lyenera^h* 68, *oğos* 149, *kordoğos* 150, *meğoria^h* 76, *konseğo* 25, *koğentes* 51, etc. The archaic spelling *-mr-* predominates over *-mbr-*, *omres* 27, *famre* 29, *nomres* 74, *nomrada^h* 53, but *sembredes* 46, *sembravan* 49.[1] Whilst the popular form in *kativos* 166 and *kativerio* 163 is adhered to, the spelling *eskribto* 62 is constantly adopted.[2]

11. The Western spelling of final *n* by *m* is shown in *segum*.[3] The fricative which Romance orthography represents by *-t, -d,* or *-th,* is transcribed by ה in words occurring at the end of a line. In the middle of a line the sound is rendered by a ד (= *d*): *atabud* 71, 84, *merçed* 68, 152. The evidence is too scanty to allow us to draw any conclusions from this practice.

12. The presence of epenthetic *-n-* in *sonsanyos* should also be mentioned here.[4]

(B) 1. The following data relating to nominal morphology should be mentioned: (*a*) The JSp form *Dio*.[5] (*b*) The etymological plural *reis*, which is exclusively used.[6] (*c*) The adjective *valiente* with desinential *-o*. This is very likely due to the assonance (comp. *doliente* 161, etc.), although in this case dialectal tendencies should be borne in mind.[7]

2. The earlier forms, *nos, vos,* of the personal pronoun seem to predominate in the language of the original over the compound ones, *nos otros, vos otros.* The latter appears twice (117, 120). Also the form *kon vusko* 168.[8]

3. Desinential *-d-* in the second person plural of the verbs is never lost: *sodes* 27, *despreçiedes* 28, *tomades* 150, *seredes* 166, etc. Imperfect *-ie* in verbs of the second and third conjugations persists in over one-third of the total number of examples. There are four instances of *-ie* (37, 53, 139, 161) against twelve of *-ia* in the third person singular. There also occurs *-iemos* 41. So that this aspect of the conjugation shows the forms in *ia* predominating over those in *ie*. As far as literary Castilian is

---

[1] Comp. *lumre, omre,* etc. Shem Tob*C* (fol. 5, 20*v* respectively), alternating with *membrara^h* ibid. 13, etc. The spelling lingers still in PConst.

[2] Also in Shem Tob*C*. Comp. *Aibto*.

[3] See 62, note. Comp. *kom*, mentioned before.

[4] See 157, note.   [5] See 58, 59, 69, 93.

[6] See 26, note.   [7] See 131, note.

[8] Comp. *kon nusko* Shem Tob*C* fol. 48*v* (*con nosotros* E fol. 68).

concerned, this points to the fourteenth century.[1] Thematic *e* in a preterite of the first conjugation appears in *gastemos*.[2] Mention also should be made at this point of the analogical *dieste* 39. In view of the rime, the form *oira*[h] 149 may be due to unintentional omission of a ᾽. It might also be taken as genuine.[3]

4. The presence of the preposition *pora*[h] 148 might indicate that the period of composition of the poem was when its use prevailed in Castile.[4]

(C) 1. The definite article is omitted before the direct object, as in 28. Also with a prepositional complement, as in 10, 84. Or with collective nouns, 24. A characteristic feature is its use with *Dio* (58, 59, 69).[5] In six instances it appears with a possessive adjective (7, 46, 47, 114, 121, 155) as against twenty-seven in which it is omitted.

2. *Nado* is used as a noun in 114. Two nouns linked by the copulative *e* may be separated by a verb, as in 76.

3. The well-known construction of descriptive adjective + *de* + noun occurs in *por malos de pekados*.[6] The noun is separated from the adjective by a verb and its subject in *la*[h] *ǧente el fizyera*[h] *toda*[h] *estar de fuera*[h] 107.[7] In *omres pastores* the second noun assumes an adjectival function.[8] The numeral is placed after the noun in 62, 87.

4. The poet is predominantly *loísta*: 75, 78, 135, etc. Comp. 91, 98, 102. In 99 there is a case of *lo* with dative. But a dittography may be suspected here, and in view of *le eran serbientes* 50, elision of *e* in *le* seems possible.[9] In 133 *las ǧentes* is used as an indefinite.[10]

5. Personal *a* with the accusative of a transitive verb is the rule: 12, 64, 73. But comp. 107. This usage is extended to non-personal accusatives: *alas tieras sembravan* 49 (comp. 46), and may be ascribed to the literal interpretation of the Hebrew Bible, which reproduces in the vernacular the *nota accusativi* אֵת. This practice is corroborated by

---

[1] Hanssen § 234.   [2] See 42, note.
[3] Whenever it occurs in Castilian texts it is a Leonesism (MPidal *Cantar* II, § 92, 4).
[4] See MPidal *Cantar* p. 363; Hanssen § 726.
[5] See 58, note.   [6] See note to 42.
[7] The position of the main verb in the phrase seems to be determined here by the internal rime.
[8] See note to 27.
[9] For *los dixera*[h], see note to 150.
[10] Comp. MPidal *Cantar* II, § 147, 2.

JSp sixteenth-century biblical translations. The construction *non pares mientes...nuestros pekados* also has parallels in later JSp.

The following features of tense usage are outstanding: (*a*) *diz* is equivalent to the perfect *dixo*, when a direct address is introduced, in 69, 165 (comp. Apol II, p. 17; JRuiz 992 d, etc.). (*b*) Pluperfect in *-ra* has its original meaning in *dixera*ʰ 105, *eǵaran* 140, etc. It is more often used, however, as a preterite (13, 15, etc.), or as a descriptive imperfect, as in *dixera*ʰ 21, 65, 121; *respondiera*ʰ 92, 112, 116. It rarely appears as a subjunctive (160). (*c*) The perfect in 15, 89, 109, 161, and the modern form of the pluperfect subjunctive in 115, are used with the meaning of a preterite.

In two instances the verb is used in the plural with a collective subject in the singular: 36, 137 (but *dezie la ǵente* 37), whilst in 24 the lack of agreement between the plural subject and the verb is obviously due to attraction by a singular complement which precedes the verb.

Pronominal interpolation between the infinitive and the auxiliary verb in the future and conditional tenses takes place in 34, 65, 67, 68, 146 and 7 (where *sakarte* is preceded by a prepositional complement). On the other hand, in 44, 69 (where the subject precedes the verb) the complement pronoun precedes the infinitive.

The interpolation of the subject between the auxiliary verb and the participle in 115 is favoured by the rime. This also accounts for the position of the auxiliary after the participle in 26, 130.

The following types of verbal paraphrase occur: (*a*) With *fazer* + noun, as in *fazer oraçion* 58; *f. ǵura*ʰ 69, 93; *f. merçed* 68, 36; *f. folia*ʰ 139; *f. buen talente* 40; *f. çerka*ʰ 135. (*b*) With *seer* + present participle, as in *s. serviente* 146, 50; *s. obediente* 99; *s. koǵente* 51. (*c*) With *aver*, as in *a. fosura*ʰ 71; *a. enoǵos* 151, etc. (*d*) With other verbs: *tomar kordoǵos* 150; *dar respuesta*ʰ 128, etc.

6. In the formation of adverbs of manner the adjective is used either alone, as *privado* 13, 81; *çierto* 27, 87; *apresurado* 126; or with *mente*, as in 31, 32, etc. Other expressions of manner with a preposition include: *de mui buen coraçon* 78; *desta*ʰ *manera*ʰ 22, 89; *en mui fuerte manera*ʰ 143; *a*ʰ *buena*ʰ *ventura*ʰ 95; *de mano* 122; *por kuenta*ʰ 159. In 19 *nunka*ʰ is used in order to stress the negation. In what I consider the original reading in 106, *ende* has a pronominal meaning (comp. 139). As an adverb of place *i* appears in 53, 144. In *di* 8 it has perhaps a pronominal function. The demonstrative particle *he* occurs in 146.

(D) 1. The position of the subject or of the complement in the phrase is often subject to metrical considerations. Thus the basis for internal rime is the verb in a great many cases. Or the main verb, if a subordinate clause is a component of the phrase. The convention by which the stanzas must end with a certain proper noun influences the construction of the phrase, particularly with regard to the position of the subject, as in 60, 72, 76, 80, 112, 156, etc. In some cases the internal rime and the compulsory ending of the stanza result in the subject and complement being placed after the verb—the latter affording an easy rime—as in 88, 92, 128, 156.

2. Apart from this, the subject is postponed to the verb whenever the phrase begins with a complement: 16, 24, 49, 98. There is indecision with regard to the imperative, as in 30, 35 (comp. 45, 96). Also with an enuntiative verb, as in *dezia*ʰ *la*ʰ *ǧente* 30, *respondia*ʰ *Yoçef* 32; but *Yoçef dixo* 45, 129.

3. In 31 the subject precedes the verb, whilst the complement is placed between subject and verb (comp. 42, 44). A complete subordinate proposition separates them in 39.

4. The complement often precedes the verb: (*a*) Direct complement without preposition, as in 9, 34, 58, etc. (*b*) With *a*ʰ, as in 11, 49, 89. (*c*) Other prepositional complements: 24, 84, 137. The determinative is placed after the verb in 51, 152. The subordinate infinitive precedes the verb in one case only (73).

VI

The metre in the present fragments may be considered as the outcome of the disintegration of the tetrastich monorime Alexandrine. Whilst the framework of the old *quaderna via* is retained, the caesura has led to the introduction of the internal rime in the traditional scheme. Thus the Alexandrine is split into two hexasyllables[1] in the great majority of cases. A uniform internal assonance or rime for the hemistichs, and another at the end of the first three lines of the stanza, is used.

From the point of view of rime arrangement, our text furnishes a parallel example to certain portions of Messire Thibaut's *Li Romanz de*

[1] In the present remarks the French system of scansion has been adopted.

la Poire.[1] Our poet, however, introduces the name of the protagonist at the end of each stanza, so that the stanza adheres to the following scheme: *ab* : *ab* : *ab* : *ac*.[2]

Taking the double line of 6 + 6 as a basis, we find that 26 out of 38 double lines, in which neither hiatus nor elision, apocope, or other similar prosodical phenomena arise, conform to the standard measure. These lines are the following:

10	28	40	45	65	82	112	145	166
24	34	42	49	72	84	114	148	168
25	38	44	55	80	97	124	155	

Of the remaining 12 double lines, one consists of 7 + 5 syllables, whilst lines 46, 48 and possibly 108 are marred by scribal errors. Eight double lines remain which are metrically unsatisfactory: 116, 128, 144, 153, 157 are of 6 + 5 syllables; whilst 35, 150, 160 are of 7 + 6, 6 + 7 and 6 + 8 syllables respectively.[3]

Hiatus is systematically used, even between identical vowels belonging to different words.[4] Taking this principle into consideration, the following lines conform to the standard measure:

5	22	32	50	63	81	95	109	125	138	151
13	27	33	52	64	83	102	113	126	140	154
14	29	39	54	71	87	103	115	130	142	162
19	30	43	61	73	88	104	121	131	146	165
20	31	47	62	74	92	107	122	134	147	

This number could be increased to 55, if the suppression suggested in line 79 were adopted.

From the spellings previously recorded in V, § 6, it is clear that along with hiatus elision was also employed. In the following passages we may

---

[1] Lines 21–240 (ed. Stehling, Halle 1881). See also the editor's remarks in his introduction, p. 27. In fourteenth-century Spanish literature there are certain metrical combinations—more or less consistently adopted— susceptible of a similar interpretation. Such are, amongst other examples, stanzas 1059–67 in the *Libro de Buen Amor*.

[2] But stanza 301 in its present state deviates from this scheme.

[3] Crasis between the final *a* of the hexasyllable and the initial of the octosyllable may be suggested in 150 (comp. FGz p. li).

[4] See Hanssen § 101. Hiatus between identical vowels must be assumed, among others, in the following lines: between *a a*, 33, 39, 122; between *e e*, 29, 39, 62, 140; between *o o*, 27, 79, 109.

surmise similar pronunciations to those shown by the spellings in the MS.: *ferm(e)as* 68, *d(e) akesta^h* 17, 117; *d(e) aki* 66, 167; *aunk(e) agora^h* 18; *desk(e) atemaba^h* 77; *s(e) adoleçia^h* 59; *m(e) ovo* 90. Crasis is also exacted by the metre in the following: *meǧoria^h avia^h* 76; *toda^h akesta^h* 164; *e enperadores* 101 (if hiatus in *reis* is assumed); *e el* and *lo obedientes* (if *lo* is genuine) 99; and either elision or crasis in *de enterar* 70, 94; *de estranyos* 158; *deske elyos* 85; *ke elyos* 86; *ke eran* 51; *sobre esto* 120; *ǧente esklamava^h* 57; *ove eredado* 110. In the following passages, however, synaloepha is required in order to obtain metrical regularity: *horo e kito* 7; *Yehuda^h enbiava^h* 11; *la ove* (if *ke* is genuine) 110; *la ovo* 15; *padre ala^h* 23; *si es* 118; *deǧarlo alyi* 132; *lo enteraran* 135; *luego a^h* 141; *lo adoraron* 143; *su ermano* (see 106, note). In 132a probably we have a dittography.

If the preceding passages are added to those previously mentioned on p. xxii we may include the following amongst the regular lines in the text:

6	23	53	67	76	89	99	118	135	149
11	26	57	68	77	90	101	120	137	158
15	37	58	69	78	91	105	123	139	167
17	41	59	70	85	93	110	129	141	
18	51	66	75	86	94	117	132	143	

To the preceding the following hexasyllables belonging to lines which are damaged in the MS. should be added: 2b, 3b, and probably also 4b, 9b, 12a, 164b.

The following lines should be read as though consisting of 7 + 5 or 5 + 7 syllables: 16, 21, 156 (with disyllabic *mui*); 60 (hiatus between *a a*); 98, 133 (synaeresis in *-iaran*); 127 (synaloepha in *muerto aki*, aphaeresis or synaloepha in *aki estava^h*).

In lines 7b, 36, 56, 106a we are confronted with errors of transmission, as is suggested in the text. In 111a, *ke* is possibly spurious.

Finally, six lines remain, which in their present state seem to be irreducible to the standard measure: four (100, 136, 152, 159) are of 6 + 5 syllables; 119b cannot be scanned in view of the state of the text; 161 is perhaps a 7 + 6 line. In conclusion, fourteen at the most, out of 160 complete lines, do not adhere to the 6 + 6, 7 + 5 or 5 + 7 scheme.

With the exception of stanzas 262, 263, 284 and 290, rime at the end of the lines is regular.[1] At the end of the first hemistichs the following

---

[1] The rime in stanzas 262, 282 shows that *b* in *Aibto* was not pronounced. The words pointed with *šureq* in ll. 6, 10 seem to indicate a rime in *-u* at the end of ll. 5, 7, 9, 11.

imperfect rimes occur : *fuerte* : *ğente* (274); *muerte* : *dieste* : *ğente* (276); *doliente* : *muerte* (309); *talente* : *siete* (282); *fuerdes* : *diredes* (267); *manda-miento* : *muerto* : *enbuelto* (287); *esto* : *çierto* : *valiento* (299). This last word possibly indicates that assonance was lacking in the original and the desinence *-o* was substituted for *-e* in order to obtain the correct assonance.[1] This also applies to *era*ʰ 106.

Such instances, when considered together with the lines in which the metrical scheme deviates from the 6 + 6 standard measure, seem to prove that the poet was writing within the compass of the *quaderna via* and the structure of the Alexandrine with a variable pause lingers in his mind.[2]

The metre thus would show the process of transition between the Alexandrine and a type of hexasyllable that would spring from it. As far as metre is concerned our poem might be related to such divided Alex-andrines as appear in the verse fragments of the *Chronica Troiana* (MS. Bca. Nac. 1-i-99)[3] or to certain distichs in the *Conde Lucanor*.[4] The com-position of the poem would then fall within the times to which these examples belong, namely the first half of the fourteenth century. Certain linguistic traits point to the thirteenth century. However, they do not seem sufficient in themselves to justify an earlier dating of the poem than the one suggested.

VII

Our poem probably originated in similar conditions to those that prompted the learned Crescas ben Joseph ha-Levi Caslari to redact a Provençal version of the story of Esther for the Purim celebrations. His avowed purpose was to provide a poetical narrative in the vernacular for those unacquainted with Hebrew.[5] That Purim narratives in the middle

---

[1] Comp. *oira*ʰ 149.

[2] Apart from the passages quoted in the previous paragraph, the punc-tuation shows that the poem might originally have been written in long lines. Whereas the punctuation mark at the end of the long lines is but once missing, it has been omitted at the end of ten first hexasyllables.

[3] A. Paz y Melia, *Poesías intercaladas en la Crónica Troyana romanceada* (RHi vi, 68, 70).

[4] Pp. 167, 249, 216 (ed. Knust). The metre in Shem Tob is susceptible of a similar interpretation.

[5] Caslari wrote two poems on the story of Esther, one in Hebrew, the other in the vernacular. In the introduction to the former work the author states that he wrote the first rendering for the benefit of women and children unacquainted with Hebrew (see Ro xxx, p. 195).

ages were not exclusively concerned with that subject is confirmed by later evidence, from the period when the so-called Purim-play took definite shape. Two of the works on Joseph mentioned before were probably written for that occasion. This is surely the case with a play concerning the sale of Joseph, by Bermann of Limburg, which was performed for the first time probably in 1713.[1]

In the Spanish lands as in Provence a certain demand for Purim narratives in the vernacular must have existed from the time when the decadence of Hebrew culture made itself felt and Jews began to write in the Peninsular Romance languages.

On the other hand, the authorship of the Provençal Esther shows that such writings do not necessarily emanate from the pen of uncultured persons. The presentation of the subject and the style of the work were suited to the audience for which they were intended. A comparison between the Hebrew and the Provençal renderings of Caslari's Esther brings out this point. The former is written in that elaborate style which characterizes medieval Hebrew poetry, whereas the latter is devoid of strictly literary features.

Our poem was intended for a public similar to that for which the Provençal Esther was written. This explains in our poem the economy of proper names. Two place names only occur. Only the more familiar names of persons are mentioned. On the other hand, Pharaoh is 'el rei'; Ἡρώων πόλις—which the *General Estoria* renders 'la çibdath delos Sennores'—is merely 'la çibdath'; Ḥushim ben Dan is 'un sordo'. Neither the land of Canaan nor the cave of Machpelah is named.[2] Such omissions are not due to ignorance, as the nature of sources used by the writer abundantly proves.

A noteworthy feature is the absence of Hebraisms in the vocabulary, if a few proper names are excepted. This is also true of the Provençal Esther. Both works contrast in this respect with other Jewish productions in the vernacular, and also with Morisco literature in general.[3]

It would be unavailing to look for literary qualities in the poem, which

[1] See I. Abrahams, *Jewish Life in the Middle Ages* (London 1932), p. 285. It would seem as if the narrative poem were the precursor of the Purim-play.

[2] Caslari makes a wider use of proper names. Thus besides 'Susan, la grant ciutat' 73, we have *Fransa, Espanha* (324), *Anglaterra* (400), *Jerusalem* (270); 'Galen o dis' (161), with reference to a well-known aphorism, etc.

[3] See Blondheim, *Poèmes Judéo-Français*, Paris 1927, pp. 33–4.

ranks decidedly lower in this respect than Caslari's production. The picturesque note, for which the latter shows a clear preference, is totally absent here. Our writer is obviously hampered by the metre, in particular by the recurrence of the same word at the end of each stanza. His expressions are plain to the point of dullness. His phraseology is monotonous and his construction at times ambiguous. The narrative has the form of a series of juxtaposed statements, and a total absence of grammatical transition is conspicuous. Sometimes a fleeting reference is made to events with which, we may assume, his audience was fully familiar. Then the text becomes a clumsily rendered abridgment of his sources.[1] Such abridgments might equally have been made from the original Hebrew source or from a vernacular version.

[1] See lines 99, 104, 129, 134–5.

TEXT
OF
COPLAS DE YOÇEF

.... ריסילון[׳] 54]

קי א... .ירני מינטיש ׳   פור לו די טו אגואילו ׳

[.ס. ניי[רין[א]רי גינטיש ׳   קום אישטריליייאש דיל סיילו ׳

אי .י. טומאר טאלינטיש ׳   קון טו [פ]... י[וסף ׳..]   4

יו קיירו דיסינדיר ׳   קונטיגו אה אאיבטו ׳

אי טי קיירו דיפינדי[ר] ׳   דישי פואיבלו [מא] דיטו ׳

2. ...קי א] The lower stroke of a ג or ם is discernible after the א. The three following letters are illegible. לו] The ו is very faint, but certain. אנגואילו] The ג is certain although its lower stroke is not clear.

3. At the beginning of the line the letter before ם might be a ﬞפ. The diacritic point is clear. The ם is very blurred. It is followed by a י or ו. ניי seems clear to me. But the second י possibly is a ו. The final י is perhaps simply a meaningless dot.

4. After אי three letters follow. The first might be an א, but at this point the page is so blurred that it is not possible to make a definite statement. Then a י follows. The third letter is completely illegible. ﬞפ...] The diacritic point and a part of the main stroke of the ﬞפ are clear. יוסף] The ו and the upper and lower ends of the ף are faintly visible.

5. Above דיסינדיר in the space between the present and the preceding stanza four letters have been added. They are written in a thick hand, not our scribe's. They reproduce the last four letters of טאלינטיש (1. 4).

6. דיפינדיר] The omission of the diacritic point on the ם is probably due to an oversight. The last three letters are much blurred. מא] Both the lower bow of מ and the upper end of ל in the ligature א are blurred. דיטוּ] The *šureq* coincides with the end of the vertical stroke of קיירו, which in the MS. falls above the ו of דיטוּ. But it seems certain.

[261] .　.　.　.　.　.　.　reçelo.

　　　Ke a...erne mientes　　Por lo de tu aguelo.

　　　.ç..ny..reare ğentes　　Kom estrelyas del çielo.

　　　E...tomar talentes　　Kon tu f[iğo] Yoçef.　　　4

[262]　Yo kiero deçender　　Kontigo a^h Aibto,

　　　E te kiero de[f]ender　　Dese pueblo mal ditu.

[261] ... fear [not. I shall bear thee (?)] in mind for the sake of
what [was promised] thy grandfather. [I shall multiply thy(?)] people as
the stars of heaven. And [now go] and rejoice (?) in Joseph, thy son.

[262] I will go down with thee into Egypt, and defend thee from that

---

1. The complete half line might have been [*E non ayas*] *reçelo*.

2. The word immediately preceding *mientes* is probably [*t*]*erne*.

3. The last three letters *-are* in the first word of this line suggest a future
indicative. The illegible word in question should mean 'to increase', 'to
multiply': *muğiguarte*, in accordance with PConst fol. 93a, 16, might have
been the primitive reading.　　*kom*: Apocope in this instance may be taken
as an indication of Leonese origin (Hanssen § 656). This form also occurs
several times in Shem Tob*C*, when both *M* and *E* have *como*, thus spoiling
the metre. See also MPidal *Cantar* p. 200; Staaff *Pronoms* p. 7.

4. *tomar talentes* 'to delight oneself'? I am unable to quote parallels.
But comp. 16. For *talente*, see Aguado, *Glosario sobre Juan Ruiz*, s.v.
This expression corresponds to כאשר ייטב בעיניך 'as it shall seem good in
thy sight' Yashar p. 183 (see full quotation below).　　*Yoçef*: I transcribe
in accordance with the Hebrew vocalization (see pp. xvi, n.; xix, n. 6).
The earliest JSp documents known to me (Aguilar de Campó, 1219, 1220)
have the form *Iuçeph* (DL nos. 23, 24). A list of other Spanish spellings
for that name may be consulted in SGFr II, 42.

5. *Aibto*: Also in Shem Tob*C*, fol. 36^v. Comp. *Agipto* Yuçuf*B* 205,
riming with *dito* (RArch vi, 25, note), as in the present stanza; *Egibto*
Alex*P* 87b; *Aifto* Grünbaum p. 13, n. 2.

6. *e te*: Read *et(e)*. 　*dese*: Comp. *deso* Shem Tob*C* fol. 35. For the
proclisis see Apol II, 7. 　 *-ditu*: On the survival of *-u* in OSp see MPidal
Or § 35, 3, where examples extending to the end of the thirteenth century
are quoted. For contemporary Leonese documents see Staaff p. 215.
Comp. *feğu* Shem Tob*C* fol. 33v. See also a Jewish will (Alba de Tormes,
1419), in RHi I, 197.

אי [ק]וניל מי פודיר ·   שקארטי יו [ה]ורו אי ק[ריט]ו ·

8 ביין דיבאש אינ[ט]ינדיר ·   לו קי [אי]..א. יוסף .׃.

[רסנ] שו ראזון אטימא[ב]א ·   א[י]ל [ש]י[נ]... וירדאדירו ·

אי נַאקֹב [קַ]אבָּאלנַאבָּה   אין קארו די [מ]אדי[רוֹ] ·

אה יהודה אינביאב[ה]   איוסף דילאנטירו ·

12 פור [ג]ושן פרי... [ט]אבה ·   יהודה אה יוסף .׃.

7. פודיר] The upper left bow of פ is very faint.   אי [אי קוניל] and ק are blurred, but certain.

8. אינטינדיר] ט is not clear.   [אי..א.] The first two letters are doubtful. Between these and the following א there is space for two letters. The letter next to the second א is illegible.

9. ראזון] The beginning of the word is faint, but certain.   [שינ...] ש and נ are not clear. There is space for three or four letters after the נ. Very faint traces of two vertical strokes suggest a ו and possibly an ר.   וירדאדירו] The initial ו is blurred at the top. The final one is perhaps pointed with a *šureq*.

10. מַאבָּאלנַאבָּה] Probably from another hand. Of the ק only the vertical stroke is partly discernible. The following א is faint, but certain.   מאדירוֹ] מ and -רוֹ are faint.

11. אינביאבה] The final ה is not legible. It is possibly an א.   איוסף] א faint.

12. פרי...טאבה] The middle of the word is completely illegible. Just under the א the ending of a נ is likely. ט is very faint.

4

E konel mi poder   Sakarte yo horo e kito.
Bien divas en[t]ender   Lo ke [e?]...a...Yoçef". 8

[263]   Su razon atemava   El [Senyor] verdadero,
E Ǧakob kavalgava^h   En karo de [m]aderu.
A^h Yehuda^h enbiava[^h]   aYoçef delantero.
Por Gosen pre...tava^h   Yehuda^h a^h Yoçef.   12

accursed nation. With my might I will bring thee out free and safe. By
this thou shalt well see that...to (?) Joseph.
[263] Thus His discourse the True Lord (?) ended, and Jacob set out on
his journey in a wooden (?) waggon. He sent Judah before him unto Joseph.
[And] Judah inquired of Joseph concerning Goshen.

7. *sakarte*: Abundant examples showing the loss of the vowel in the
pronoun, when proclitic to *e, emos, as, an, ie*, etc., may be seen in SGFr II,
64. This is not an exclusively Leonese feature, as it occurs in Mio Cid,
Berceo, Apolonio, as well as in JRuiz*S*, Alex *P*, and later MSS.   *yo*: In
view of the metre it seems to be an addition (comp. 65,.67, 68). I would
read *sakarte (yo) horo e kito*.   *horo*: Comp. *alforria* 'freedom, emancipation', in BFerrar (MLN xi, col. 34).   *kito*: Usual (MPidal *Cantar*
p. 177; III, s.v. Milagr 77b, passim; Apol II, s.v.; JRuiz 300, etc.). The
expression *horo e kito* seems equivalent to *libre e quito* in legal documents
(DL no. 320, 10, etc.).

8. דיבאש] The deterioration of the text at this spot renders interpretation difficult. The original reading stands perhaps for *d'i vas*: comp.
por hi MCid 3607 (MPidal *Cantar* II, § 134, 3), SGFr I, 11, 8; *de y* PCG
466a, 38. See Hanssen § 624. But we may read *de vas* in view of Yuçuf*A*
60b (comp. RArch vi, 289), VTristan 115, 17, and passim.

9. *atemava*: The verb *atemar*, as it is well known, persists in JSp, and
in late Arabic *aljamiado* texts alternates with *atamar*, which is well attested
otherwise in fourteenth and fifteenth century literary works, such as
JRuiz 857b, BAlba I, p. 89, CBaena p. 140, etc. Also in Shem Tob*C* fol. 38
(*acabar* ME).   *senyor verdadero*: Also in Yuçuf*B* 51b.

10. *kavalgava^h en karo*: Comp. JRuiz 1219c.   *karo de maderu*: I am
unable to quote parallels. Biblical versions do not help (comp. BAlba p. 88;
BEsc p. 63b, BFerrar fol. 23a, in the corresponding passage, Gen 46, 5).

11. *delantero*: Comp. "e a Juda enbio el adelante a Yosep" BEsc
p. 64a; "y a Yehudah embio delante del a Yoseph" BFerrar fol. 23a.

12. Probably *pre[gun]tava^h*, i.e. 'Judah inquired of Joseph concerning
Goshen'.

5

דישקי יא לו שופ̄יירה ·   יוסף̄ מוי פ̄ריואדו ·

אה ריסיביר שאיירה ·   אשו פדרי אונראדו ·

לה מאנו לי פידיירה ·   לואיגו לה אובֹו בישאדו ·

מוי גראן פ̄לאזיר אוביירה ·   גֿאקוב קון יוסף̄ ·.·   16

גֿאקוב לואיגו דיזיאה ·   ביין די אקישטה [מ]נירה ·   רסה

וִישטֹו אֵי אֵינריאה ·   אאון קי אגורה מואירה ·

קי יו נונקה שביאה ·   קי יוסף̄ ביבֹו אירה ·

פ̄לאזיר אי אישטי דיאה ·   קון מי פֿיגֿו יוסף̄ ·.·   20

יוסף̄ לי דישירה ·   קון מוי גראן אומילדאת ·   רסו

דירי דישטה מנירה ·   אֵל ריאי פֿור וירדאת ·

קומו וינידו אירה ·   מי פדרי אֵלֹה סיבדאת ·

אי קי קונֵיל ויניירה ·   אֵ[י]רמנוש די יוסף̄ ·.·   24

14. [ריסיביר] The second י consists of two dots. They are very close together, so as to be scarcely distinguishable from each other. A single letter is undoubtedly meant. Comp. ll. 18, 26, 105.

17. [מנירה] The scribe wrote נ instead of מ, possibly due to attraction by the final letter of the preceding word. It is obvious that מ was meant.

18. The usual dot denoting the end of a hemistich or line is here a stroke after the ה of אינריאה. [וִישטֹו] There are two dots at the end of the word: a meaningless one at the top left of the ו, while the other is clearly a *šureq*. The *ḥireq* falls under the י. [אֵינריאה] The first י appears to be written by two dots. On close examination of the MS. it becomes clear that the two dots are joined, and consequently stand for one single letter. [אאון קי] A dot on the top left of the first א seems meaningless.

19. [ביבֹו] The ו is very faint, but certain.

21. [דישירה] The diacritic point occurs here on the ש.

24. [אירמנוש] A letter, probably another י after אי-, has been subsequently deleted.

[264] Deske ya lo sopieraʰ   Yoçef mui privado
A ʰ reçebir salieraʰ   Asu padre onrado.
Laʰ mano le pidieraʰ;   Luego laʰ ovo besado.
Mui gran plazer obieraʰ   Ğakob kon Yoçef.   16

265   Ğakob luego deziaʰ   Bien de akestaʰ [m]aneraʰ:
"Vistu e alegriaʰ,   Aun ke agoraʰ mueraʰ!
Ke yo nunkaʰ sabiaʰ   Ke Yoçef bivo eraʰ:
Plazer e este diaʰ   Kon mi fiğo Yoçef".   20

266   Yoçef le dixeraʰ   Kon mui gran omildath:
"Dire destaʰ maneraʰ   Al rei por verdath,
Komo venido eraʰ   Mi padre alaʰ çibdath,
E ke konel vinieraʰ   Ermanos de Yoçef.   24

[264] [And] since Joseph knew of his coming, he arose quickly and went forth to meet his worthy father. He asked for his hand and kissed it. Jacob delighted exceedingly in Joseph.

265. Then well spake Jacob in this wise: "Joy have I seen even were I now to die, for I knew not that Joseph was alive. Pleased I am to-day with Joseph, my son".

266. With great humility thus spake Joseph unto him: "To the king thus truly I shall say how my father has come unto the city and with him Joseph's brethren.

13. *privado* 'quickly': Usual (see MPidal *Cantar* p. 180, 5).

15. *pidieraʰ*: The pretonic here and in other similar cases is transcribed *i* in accordance with the pointing of the MS. in ll. 105, 131.

19. *nunkaʰ sabiaʰ*: On *nunca* merely reinforcing the negation, see Wagenaar p. 86.

20. *este diaʰ*: See MPidal *Cantar* III, s.v. *dia*.

22. *destaʰ*: Comp. *dese* 6.   *por verdath* 'truly'. On modal *por*, see MPidal *Cantar* p. 187, 5; Apol II, s.v.; SGFr II, 59.

24. *konel vinieraʰ ermanos*: See for this construction SGFr II, 93–5.

[רסז] מי קונשיג֗ו טומידיש ・ מיש אירמנוש מיורִיש ・

שי פריגונטאדוש פֿואירדיש ・ די ריאיש או די שיניורִיש ・

קי שֹודֵיש וֹש דירידיש ・ סירטו אומריש פֿאשטורִיש ・

אי ווש נון דישפריסיידִיש ・ קֻונשיג֗ו די יוסף ・.・   28

. . . .
. . . .
. . . .
. . . .

[רעד] לא פֿאמרי אירה פֻֿואירטִי ・ שוברי טודה לה טיירה ・

אי דיזיאה לה ג֗ינטִי ・ יוסף דאנוש סיבִירה ・

קי פלאטה סירטה מינטִי ・ אטי יא דאדה אירה ・

אפרישוראדה מינטִי ・ ריישפונדיאה יוסף ・.・   32

רעה לה פלאטה קי טינידִיש ・ שי אירה אטימאדה ・

לוש קאבאליוש מי דידִיש ・ אי דר ווש אי סֻואדה ・

---

26. פריגונטאדוש] The י consists of two dots, which on close examination are seen to be joined, thus forming one letter. Comp. l. 14.

27. שֹודֵיש] The ṣere is faint, but certain.

28. The lacuna is obvious from the marginal numbering of the stanzas. Judging from the context six stanzas are missing, although there is no indication of a gap at this point. It seems plausible to conclude that the scribe was copying from a MS. which contained about three stanzas on a page, and from that MS. a leaf was missing after our present l. 28.

32. ריישפונדיאה] There is a meaningless dot on the פ.

33. The number רעה in the margin was wrongly written ערה by the scribe. The obvious transposition is indicated by dots over the letters affected.

[267] Mi konseǧo tomedes,   Mis ermanos mayores:
   Si preguntados fuerdes   De reis o de senyores,
   Ke sodes, vos diredes,   Çierto omres pastores:
   E vos non despreçiedes   Konseǧo de Yoçef".   28

  .　　.　　.　　.　　.　　.　　.　　.　　.
  .　　.　　.　　.　　.　　.　　.　　.　　.
  .　　.　　.　　.　　.　　.　　.　　.　　.
  .　　.　　.　　.　　.　　.　　.　　.　　.

[274] La^h famre era^h fuerte   Sobre toda^h la^h tiera^h;
   E dezia^h la^h ǧente: "Yoçef, danos çibera^h!
   Ke plata^h çierta^h mente   Ati ya dada^h era^h".
   Apresurada^h mente   Respondia^h Yoçef: 32

275 "La plata^h ke tenedes,   Si era^h atemada^h,
   Los kabalyos me dedes,   E dar vos e çevada^h".

[267] Ye my elder brethren, pay heed unto my counsel: Should ye be asked by kings or rulers what ye are, then shall ye answer that surely ye are shepherds. And Joseph's advice despise ye not".

  .　　.　　.　　.　　.　　.　　.　　.

[274] The famine was sore in all the land. And the people said: "Joseph, give us bread! The money indeed to thee was given". And straightway Joseph answered:

275. "If your money fail, bring me your horses, and I shall give ye food."

26. *reis*: The etymological form of the plural occurs in Castile as late as the last decade of the fourteenth century (DL no. 300, 16). See also SGFr I, 21, 2, and passim.

27. *omres pastores*: The adjectival function of the second noun might have originated from האנשים רעי צאן ('the men are shepherds') + אנשי מקנה ('men of cattle'), Gen 46, 33–4. Comp. MPidal *Cantar* II, p. 121. For the spelling -*mr*- see p. xxiii.

29. *fuerte*: It is the Hebr. כבד (Gen 43, 1), rendered *grave* and *pesgada* by BFerrar and PConst respectively.

9

ישׁ

[רעו]

36

40

44

דישׁירון וושׁ לושׁ טומידישׁ ‏ ‏ לה ‏"גﬞינטי דישׁיאדה ‏

אינטינדיאן קי מירסידישׁ ‏ ‏ לישׁ פﬞאזיאה יוסף ‏∴

דישׁפﬞואישׁ דיזיאי לה גﬞינטי ‏ ‏ קומו לה ויז פרימירה ‏

אישׁקאפﬞאנושׁ די מואירטי ‏ ‏ יוסף דאנושׁ סיבﬞירה ‏

קי איל פﬞאן קי נושׁ דיישׁטי ‏ ‏ יא אטימאדו אירה ‏

פﬞאז נושׁ בﬞואין מאלינטי ‏ ‏ נון מוראמושׁ יוסף ‏∴

לה פלאטה קי טיניﬞמושׁ ‏ ‏ אוטרושׁי לושׁ גנאדושׁ ‏

נושׁ טודו לו גﬞאשׁטימושׁ ‏ ‏ פﬞור מאלושׁ די פיקאדושׁ ‏

לאשׁ טייראשׁ קי אבﬞימושׁ ‏ ‏ אי לושׁ קואירפﬞושׁ קוטאדושׁ ‏

נושׁ טודו לו דארימושׁ ‏ ‏ פﬞור סיויירה יוסף ‏∴

35. דישׁירון] The diacritic mark of the שׁ, which in the present instance is similar to the strokes used in numerals and abbreviations, is placed here above and between the following י and ר. לושׁ] The שׁ has been subsequently added, either by the copyist or by another hand very much like his.

37. קומו] There is a meaningless dot below the מ.

38. מואירטי] A dot follows -אי-. It falls immediately above the curve of the ר. יוסף] There is a meaningless dot over the י.

40. After מאלינטי a dash separates the hemistichs. Probably it belongs to an unfinished letter started in the wrong place.

Dixeron: "Vos los tomedes".   La ǧente dese[s]ada^h
Entendian ke merçedes   Les fazia^h Yoçef.   36

276   Despues dezie la ǧente: "Komo la^h vez primera^h,
Eskapanos de muerte,   Yoçef, danos çivera^h!
Ke el pan ke nos dieste,   Ya atemado era^h.
Faz nos buen talente,   Non muramos, Yoçef!   40

[277]   La plata^h ke teniemos,   Otrosi los ganados,
Nos todo lo gastemos,   Por malos de pekados:
Las tieras ke avemos   E los kuerpos kuitados,
Nos todo lo daremos   Por çivera^h, Yoçef!"   44

They said: "Take them". The distraught people understood that Joseph dealt kindly with them.

276. Later the people said: "Save us from death as before, O Joseph, give us bread! The bread that thou gavest us is already consumed. Show to us a kindly face, that we perish not, O Joseph!"

[277] "The money that was ours, our cattle as well, we have all consumed, for [our] wretched sins. Our lands and wretched bodies, for food we shall give thee, O Joseph!"

35. *la ǧente dese[s]ada^h*: Comp. "e andavan desvariados los de la tierra de Egipto con la fanbre" BAlba p. 89. "I enlokesiose tiera de Miṣrayim" PConst fol. 91a (Gen 47, 13). *Desesado* 'maddened', as in Milagr 193a.

36. The metre would require an imperfect in -*ie* (*fazie*), or -*ien* (*entendien*) in this line; or else synaeresis in either of these words as they stand.

38. *eskapanos*: escapar 'to free from a danger' (MPidal *Cantar* III, s.v.). Comp. Apol 165c. "E noš emoš mi^yedo ke noš perderemoš en akešta eškurida: eškapanoš della" RAlex fol. 93. "Ruegote que escapes mi alma" in a fifteenth century JSp liturgy (BAH xxxiii, 86).

39. *dieste*: See Gassner p. 156; SGFr II, 101.

40. *faz nos buen talente* 'show a good disposition towards us'.

42. *gastemos*: For the thematic vowel, see Gassner p. 134; Staaff p. 293; SGFr II, ibid. *por malos de pekados*: Comp. Apol 100c, Yuçuf*A* 19d. See Hanssen § 473.

יוסף דישׂו טומידיש ·   טודוש מוגֿה סיוירה ·

אי לואינו שימברידיש ·   טודה לה וואישטרה טי(ו)ירה · 56]

אי איל קינטו דארידיש ·   דילה וואישטרה סיוירה ·

אי שיימפרי מאנטירנידיש ·   פֿואירו די יוסף .ׁ. 48

אלאש טיראש שימבראבֿאן ·   טודאש אקישטאש גֿינטיש ·

אי דילנטיל אישטאבֿאן   אי לי איראן שירבֿיינטיש ·

אי איל קינטו לי דאבֿאן ·   די לו קי איראן קוגֿינטיש ·

אי איל פֿואירו אושאבֿאן ·   קי ליש פושו יוסף .ׁ. 52

[רפ] אבֿי אי אונה טיירה ·   די מונאדגֿוש נומראדה ·

אי אאילוש ליש דיירה ·   מאש נון פֿואי בראטאדה ·

---

46. טיירה] The scribe by mistake wrote סיוירה by attraction to the preceding or the following line. Then the ס was struck out and a ט was written above in the margin, probably by the same hand. The ו between the two יי was left, but there is no doubt that טיירה was intended to be the final reading.

49. אלאש] A dot is just visible close to the upper stroke of the first א. The upper stroke of the ל is unusually thick, showing that it has been gone over again, whether by our scribe or by another hand it is impossible to say.

50. שירבֿיינטיש] A dot is faintly visible above the second י, but this is not certain.

278 Yoçef dixo: "Tomedes Todos muğa^h çivera^h,

  E luego sembr[ar]edes Toda^h la^h vuestra^h tiera^h;

  E el kinto daredes Dela^h vuestra^h çivera^h,

  E siempre manternedes [El] fuero de Yoçef". 48

279 Alas tieras sembravan Todas akestas ğentes,

  E delantel estavan E le eran serbientes,

  E el kinto le davan De lo ke eran koğentes,

  E el fuero usaban Ke les puso Yoçef. 52

[280] Abie i una^h tiera^h De mona(d)gos nomrada^h,

  E aelyos les diera^h —Mas non fue baratada^h

---

278. Joseph said: "Corn in plenty shall ye take, and your land ye shall sow. And the fifth part of your corn ye shall give. And for all time Joseph's statute shall ye keep".

279. And all the people sowed the lands. They did remain before him and were his servants. And they gave unto him the fifth part of all they gathered. Thus they did abide by the statute which Joseph laid upon them.

[280] A famous land there was belonging unto priests. To them were

---

49. *alas tieras*: On the use of *a* in the present instance, see intr. p. xxiv. Comp. "he compre a vos oy y a vuestras tierra a Parho. He a vos simiente y sembraredes a la tierra" BFerrar fols. 23 d–24 a (Gen 47, 26). See ZRPh xxx, 180.

50. *le eran serbientes*: *serbientes* corresponds to Hebr. עבדים (Gen 47, 25). Comp. BFerrar fol. 24 a, 10.

51. *eran koğentes*: It is the Hebr. construction היה + participle = imperfect (see ZRPh xxx, 181). *koğentes*: On the absorption of *i* when it occurs in the diphthong *ie*, by a preceding palatal, see MPidal *Cantar* II, § 36, 7g.

53. *monagos*: Comp. "de çierto tierra de monagos non compro" PConst fol. 96 v. The form *monadgo* of the scribe is otherwise unknown to me. The *-d-* seems to be due to a confusion with the suffix *-adgo*. See SGFr II, 17.

54-5. *E aelyos les diera^h Mas non fue baratada^h Por pan e por çivera^h Sienpre kosa^h tağada^h*. The construction of these lines as it stands seems hardly possible. A transposition of the hemistichs might be assumed on

פור פֿאן אי פֿור סיבֿירה · שיינפֿרי קושה טאגֿאדה ·
מאש אאיליוש נון פֿואירה · פֿואירו די יוסף ·:·

[רפֿא]   [56ע]
יוסף קואנדו ויאיאה · קי לה גֿינטי אישקלאמאבֿה ·
גרנדי אורסיון פֿויאה · אי אל דין אלאבבֿה[ן·]
איל דין שי אדוליסיאה · אי לא פֿאמרי [טי]ראבֿה ·
מגֿירה אאון טיניאה · סיוירה יוסף ·:·
60

[רפֿב]
גֿאקוב אשו טאלינטי · אישטידו אין אאיבטו ·
אניוש דייז אי שיטי · שיגֿום קי איש אישקריבטו ·
שובֿרי לה אוטרה גֿינטי · אויאה מיגֿור ויטו ·
אה אורה די שו מואירטי · לייאמו איל אה יוסף ·:·
64

56. מאש] An א was first intended, then emended to מ.
58. אורסיון] The ס is blurred, but certain.
59. טיראבֿה] ט and בֿה- are blurred, and the י פֿאמרי] מרי- is blurred. almost illegible.

Por pan e por çivera^h— Sienpre kosa^h taǧada^h;
Mas aelyos non fuera^h [El] fuero de Yoçef. 56

[281] Yoçef kuando veia^h Ke la ǧente esklamava^h,
Grande oraçion fazia^h E al Dio alabava^h.
El Dio se adoleçia^h E la famre tirava^h,
Magera^h aun tenia^h Çivera^h Yoçef. 60

[282] Ǧakob asu talente Estido en Aibto
Anyos diez e siete, Segum ke es eskribto;
Sobre la^h otra^h ǧente Avia^h meǧor vito.
A^h ora^h de su muerte Lyamo el a^h Yoçef. 64

always assigned their allotted portions. But the land was not sold for bread or other food. And Joseph's statute did not apply to them.

[281] Joseph when he saw that the people were crying [in distress], in deep earnest prayed he and glorified God. God had compassion on them and caused the famine to cease, though Joseph still had food in his keeping.

[282] And Jacob abode at his ease in the land of Egypt seventeen years, as it is written. He had better meat than the rest of the people. As he drew nigh unto death for Joseph he called.

the part of the scribe, but the order of the MS. has been kept in the present edition, though *Por pan e por çivera^h Mas non fue baratada^h, E aelyos les diera^h Sienpre kosa^h taǧada^h* may be possible. (For *mas* 'never', see MPidal *Cantar* III, s.v. Wagenaar pp. 96, 99.) Another solution would be: *Mas por pan e por çivera^h Non fue baratada^h*, thus altering to 7 + 5 the structure of line 54. *kosa^h taǧada^h*: 'portion, allowance'. Comp. "les davan delos çilleros de Pharaon alos saçerdotes cosa estaiada pora sus espensas" GEst 243 b.

57. *Yoçef*: Perhaps should read *Ǧakob*. See p. 42, note *in loc*.

58. *grande oraçion*: Read *grand(e)*. Comp. 76. *al Dio*: The article here is probably a hebraism (Ro xlix, p. 40). But this practice is not restricted to JSp texts (see VTristan 8).

60. *magera^h*: Comp. JRuizS 749 d. See Hanssen § 688.

61. *estido*: See Gassner p. 156, MPidal *Cantar* p. 283.

62. *segum*: A Leonese spelling. Also in Shem Tob*C* fol. 1 (*segun* E). See Staaff p. 248, MPidal *Cantar* p. 269. *eskribto*: This spelling is constant in Shem Tob*C*. It occurs in Arabic *aljamiado*, as in RAlex fols. 1, 122, etc.

די זירטי קום פֿאראש ·   גֿאקוב לואיגו דישירה ·   [רפג]

די אקי מי ליבֿאראש ·   דישקי אגורה מואירה

אלייא מי שוטיראראש ·   ליבֿארמאש אה מי טיירה ·

שי לו פֿאזיש יוסף ׃   פֿירמיאש מירסיד ליינירה ·   68 [57

איניל דין די לוש סיילוש ·   דין טו מי פֿאראש גֿורה ·   [רפד]

דו יאזין מיש אגואילוש ·   די אינטרארר מי פֿיגורה ·

מי אטאבֿוד אינטריליוש ·   אי קי אייא פושורה ·

לי גֿוראבֿה יוסף ׃   לואיגו פור שו מישורה ·   72

אטודראש שוש קונפֿנייאש ·   גֿאקוב לייאמר פֿזיאה ·   רפה

נומריש די אימאנייאש ·   אי לואיגו ליש פונייאה ·

די מוי מוגֿאש קאלאנייאש ·   אי איל לוש וינדיזיאה ·

אי בֿינדיסין יוסף ׃   גֿראן מיגֿוריאה אוייאה ·   76

68. פֿאזיש] Besides the diacritic mark, the פ has a dash perpendicular to the upper horizontal stroke. It is perhaps the beginning of another letter, subsequently rejected by the scribe.

70. אינטרארר] The omission of the י after the ט is a lapsus (cf. l. 94). פֿיגורה] The point above the פ is faint.

71. פושורה] There is a very faint dash over the פ, scarcely discernible in the rotograph. Neither its position nor its shape justifies its being interpreted as a diacritic mark.

72. מישורה] A ו was written by mistake instead of ש, and subsequently emended by the scribe. גֿוראבֿה] The diacritic point belonging to the גֿ appears above the following ו.

75. Between איל and לוש, אנוש was first written and subsequently crossed out.

16

[283] Ǧakob luego dixera^h: "Dezirte kom faras
Deske agora^h muera^h: De aki me levaras;
Levarmas a^h mi tiera^h; Alya me soteraras.
Fermeas merçed lyenera^h Si lo fazes, Yoçef". 68

[284] Diz: "Tu me faras ǧura^h Enel Dio de los çielos,
De ent[e]rar mi figura^h Do yazen mis aguelos,
E ke aya [f]osura^h Mi atabud entrelyos".
Luego, por su mesura^h, Le ǧuraba^h Yoçef. 72

285 Ǧakob lyamar fazia^h Atodas sus konpanyas,
E luego les ponia^h Nomres de alimanyas,
E el los vendezia^h De mui muǧas kalanyas.
Gran meǧoria^h avia^h E vendiçion Yoçef. 76

[283] Then Jacob said unto him: "I shall tell thee what thou shalt do when now I die: Thou shalt bear me unto my country, and there shalt thou bury me. Shouldst thou do this, O Joseph, thou shalt deal full kindly with me".
[284] And he said: "Swear unto me by the God of Heaven that thou wilt lay my body in the burying place of my fathers, that with them my coffin may be buried". Then, as behoved him did Joseph swear unto him.
285. Jacob called unto his people, and he named them with the names of the beasts. And he did bestow upon them divers blessings. And Joseph was greatly favoured and blessed [above the others].

65. *dezirte*: On *dezir* 'to ask', see SGFr II, 42.

68. *fermeas merçed lyenera^h*: It is the ועשית חסד עמדי ואמת (Gen 47, 29) which BFerrar fol. 24a renders "y haras comigo merçed y verdad", this last noun being rendered by an adjective in the present text. *llenero* is well known in medieval texts (Apol 44c, JRuiz 513b, etc.).

69. *diz*: Comp. 165. *me faras ǧura^h*: Comp. JRuiz 660c. See MPidal *Cantar* III, s.v. *iura*.

71. *fosura^h*: 'interment'. The suffix may be due to analogy with *sepultura*. Comp. *foxal* YuçufA 45c; *fonsarios* BEsc p. 67 (Gen 47, 30); JRuizT 1554b. *atabud*: Comp. MPidal *Infantes* p. 438.

72. *por su mesura^h*: Comp. FGz 111c, Apol II, s.v.

73. *konpanyas*: Comp. MPidal *Cantar* III, s.v. GEst 260a, 2, passim.

76. *meǧoria^h*: Comp. Apol II, s.v. JRuiz 1247b, YuçufA 5d.

גאקוב דישקי אטימאבה ·   די דיזיר שו ראזון ·

אי איל לוש קונשיגֿנאבה ·   די מוי "בואין קוראסון ·

אי לואיגו איל שי פראבֿה ·   פֿאזיינדו אורסיון ·

80   אי יא לואיגו בישאבה ·   אשו פדרי יוסף ·.·.

רפז   יוסף שו מאנדֿאמיינטו ·   פֿיזו מוי פריאדו ·

פֿיזו ואנייאר אֿל מוארטו ·   לואיגו פֿואי פֿימינטאדו ·

דישפֿואיש פֿואירה אינבואילטו ·   אין און פאניו אונראדו ·

84   אין אטאבוד פֿואי פֿואישטו ·   קומו מנדו יוסף ·.·.

78. [קונשיגֿנאבה] The diacritic point over בֿ is very faint.

79. [איל] A dot, apparently meaningless, is visible under the right ending of the א.   [פראבֿה] The ר is blurred. Its shape is very similar to a ד.   [אורסיון] Both the ר and the lower stroke of ס are blurred.

80. [אשו] The ו is very short, and can easily be mistaken for a י.

81. [פֿיזו] The diacritic mark may be here a short stroke like an acute accent.   [פריאדו] The ר is partly blurred, and a point is faintly discernible close to the ו.

82. [פֿיזו] The diacritic point is faint.   [פֿואי] The diacritic mark may be similar to that of פֿ in פֿואירטי 29 and פֿאזיש 68. One dash at least above the פ is visible. After פֿואי the scribe wrote a מ, which he then crossed out.

18

[286]   Ǧakob deske atemaba^h   De dezir su razon
        E el los konseǧava^h   De mui buen koraçon,
        (E) luego el se pa[s]ava^h   Faziendo oraçion.
        E ya luego besava^h   Asu padre Yoçef.   80

287   Yoçef su mandamiento   Fizo mui priado.
        Fizo vanyar al muerto;   Luego fue pimentado;
        Despues fuera^h enbuelto   En un panyo onrado.
        En atabud fue puesto,   Komo mando Yoçef.   84

[286] And Jacob when he had made an end of speaking and had with good heart counselled them, gave up the ghost while he was yet praying. And then Joseph kissed his father.

287. Joseph his father's commandment quickly fulfilled: the dead body he ordered to be bathed; then it was embalmed. After, in a rich cloth it was wrapped. In a coffin it was laid, as Joseph commanded.

79. *pasava*^h: The reading *parava*^h in the MS. is a scribal error. *pasarse* 'to be dying' occurs in Alex*P* 173 a: "Ya tornava los ojos e passar se queria, Contendio con el alma, que transido jazia". BFerrar and PConst translate ויגוע in the source of the present passage (Gen 49, 33) by *transiose*. At the beginning of the present line, *e* is probably due to attraction by the preceding or the following lines.

81. *mandamiento*: Hebr. מצוה. *priado*: It is current in fourteenth to sixteenth-century texts. Comp. Shem Tob*C* fol. 29 (also in *E* fol. 46*v*), but *privado* M, fol. 73. The same hesitation prevails in the MSS. of JRuiz. See MPidal *Cantar* p. 180.

82. *vanyar*: The same spelling occurs in GEst 256 b, 52; 257 a, 5, and passim. *fue pimentado*: *pimentar* 'to embalm'. It is unknown to me in Sp texts. But with a prefix is well known in OFr: "L'abes a fait li cors gentement conreer....D'aloes et de myre le fait empimenter" Ste Euphrosyne 61 (Godefroy, s.v. *empimenter*).

83. *onrado*: 'excellent, precious'. See MPidal *Cantar* III, s.v. *ondrado*.

דישקי איליוש אטימאבֿאן ·   די אינֿאר לה פֿמיינטה ·   רפח

גֿינטיש אאיל ליוראבֿאן ·   קי איליוש איראן שין קואינטה ·

איניל לייאנטו טוראבֿאן ·   סיירטו דיאש שיטינטה ·

קי מוגֿו לו אמאבֿאן ·   טודוש קום איוסף ·.·   88

יוסף דישטה מנירה ·   אל ריאי אובֿו פֿבלאדו ·   [רפט]   [58]

מי פֿדרי מי דישֿירה ·   אי מי אובֿו קונגֿוראדו ·

קי לי ליבֿאשי אשו טיירה ·   דישקי פֿואישי [פֿ]ינאדו ·

אי לואיגו רישפֿונדיירה ·   איל ריאי אה יוסף ·.·   92

שי טו פֿיזישטי גֿורה ·   איניל דיו די לוש סילוש ·   רצ

די אינטיראר שו פֿיגורה ·   דו אישטאבֿן שוש אגֿואילוש ·

וֵי אה בואינה וינטורה ·   אינטיירֿאלו אינטרילייוש ·

אי לואיגו פֿור טו מישורה ·   טורנאטי יוסף ·.·   96

---

86. גֿינטיש] The diacritic point over ג has been carelessly omitted.

91. פֿינאדו] The diacritic is not clear. In the rotograph a dash, almost a continuation of the upper hook of the פ, is faintly visible, but it might be simply a part of the ן of ריסיבֿיירון 101. If this is so the diacritic has been omitted.

94. אגֿואילוש] The א is blotted, but otherwise certain.

95. וֵי] The *ṣere* is faintly visible, but it is certain.

96. טו] The lower end of the ט is blurred.

20

288   Deske elyos atemavan   De eğar la^h pimienta^h,
       Ğentes ael lyoravan   Ke elyos eran sin kuenta^h;
       Enel lyanto turavan   Çierto dias setenta^h,
       Ke muğo lo amavan   Todos kom aYoçef.   88

[289]   Yoçef desta^h manera^h   Al rei ovo fablado:
       "Mi padre me dixera^h   E me ovo konğurado
       Ke le levase asu tiera^h   Deske fuese finado".
       E luego respondiera^h   El rei a^h Yoçef: 92

290   "Si tu feziste ğura^h   Enel Dio de los çielos,
       De enterar su figura^h   Do estavan sus aguelos,
       Ve a^h buena^h ventura^h;   Entieralo entrelyos,
       E luego, por tu mesura^h,   Tornate, Yoçef".   96

288. When they had made an end of the embalming, numberless people mourned him. Seventy days indeed they mourned him, as they loved him exceedingly as they loved Joseph.

[289] Joseph in this wise to the king spake: "My father did command me and made me swear that I would take [his bones] to the land [of his fathers] when he should have yielded up his spirit". And then the king answered unto Joseph:

290. "If thou didst swear on oath by the God of Heaven that thou wouldst bury his body in the resting place of his fathers, go up, and God speeding thee, lay him in their midst, and then, as behoves thee, return, O Joseph".

85. *pimienta^h*: Unattested to my knowledge in OSp in the meaning of 'spices'.

86. *ğentes...ke elyos*: Comp. "et las gentes van nudos" MPolo 92, 93. On the syntactical function of *ke* in constructions like the present one, see SGFr II, 30. *ğentes*, lit. 'people', may also be 'gentiles'. Comp. Gen. 50, 11.

91. *ke le levase*: Read *kel(e) levas(e)*. Otherwise synaloepha should be assumed between *levase* and *asu*. Comp. *pued, tien, konvien*, etc. Shem TobC fol. 6v; *el kes metio* ibid. fol. 41.

94. *enterar*: Comp. 70.

שו קאמינו גישאבֿאן ·   יוסף אי שוש שירויינטיש ·   [רצא]

אאיל לי אקומפנייאבֿאן ·   אוטראש מוגֿאש גֿינטיש ·

אייל קאמינו פראבֿאן   פור שיאירלו אובֿידיינטיש ·   [58v]

א[ה] גֿאקוב אואינאבֿאן ·   טודוש קון יוסף ׃.·   100

א מואירטו ריסיבֿיירון ·   ריאיש אי אינפיראדוריש ·   [רצב]

אי לי אובֿידיסיירון ·   קומו בואינוש שיניוריש ·

דירידור לי פֿושיירון ·   קורונאש די אונוריש ·

אקישטו דיקוגֿירון ·   לוש ריאיש די יוסף ׃.·   104

97. שׁוּשׁ] There is a barely visible dot on the וֹ, which I scarcely think is meant to be a vocalic point.

99. אאיל] The second א is practically undistinguishable from ג. A close study of the scribe's hand convinces me that א, not ג, is intended. At first no difference is perceptible between this letter and the medial ג of אואינאבֿאן in the following line, except for a slight angular shape in the present one. This detail characterizes one of the varieties of א in the MS. On the other hand the present letter is shorter than an ordinary א. שיאיר] There is a dot below the א. It does not seem intended as a vocalic point.

100. אה] An א instead of ה was first written. The dot indicating the end of a line has been placed by mistake after this word instead of the preceding one.

102. קומו] The ו seems at first as if it were written across the left stroke of the מ. On closer examination, however, it becomes clear that the excessive length of the ן of ריסיבֿיירון in the preceding line compelled the scribe to go over the left portion of the מ and the ו again, in order to avoid confusion. Thus these strokes were thickened and appear as a single oblique stroke.

22

[291] Su kamino gisavan   Yoçef e sus servientes;
     Ael le akompanyavan   Otras muğas ğentes;
     Eel kamino paravan   Por seer lo obedientes.
     Aʰ Ğakob oinavan   Todos kon Yoçef.   100

[292] Al muerto reçebieron   Reis e enperadores,
     E le obedeçieron   Komo buenos senyores;
     Deredor le pusieron   Koronas de onores:
     Akesto dekoğeron   Los reis de Yoçef.   104

[291] Joseph and his servants made ready for their journey. Many other people did accompany him. To do him homage they did prepare the way, and together with Joseph mourned they all for Jacob.

[292] The corps was received by kings and emperors. And as befitting loyal lords showed him homage and surrounded him with [their] crowns of majesty. And this [act of homage] the kings learned from Joseph.

97. *gisavan*: *guisar* 'to make preparations'. Usual. Comp. GEst 259 b, 56.

99. *por seer lo obedientes*: On *lo* dative, see Ro xxiv, 109–11; MPidal *Cantar* I, § 130, 2.

100. *oinavan*: *oinar* 'to lament'. Also in BFerrar fol. 25 b, 8; and PConst fol. 98 a, 16 (Gen 50, 10), whereas BEsc p. 69 uses *llantear* instead.

103. *koronas de onores*: *onor* seems to correspond here to כבוד, which means both 'honour' and 'majesty'.

104. *dekoğeron*: *dekoğer* 'to learn'. Comp. "Oviste buen maestro, sopot bien castigar, Tu bien lo decolliste, como buen escolar" AlexP 219; "Esfuerço e franqueza fue luego decogiendo" ibid. 12.

23

[רצג] יוסף טודו לו פֿיזְיֵירה ·   קומו איל פֿדרי דישֿירה ·

עשו שו אירמנו אי אירה ·   קונטראליאדור לי פֿואירה ·

לה גינטי איל פֿיזיירה ·   טודה אישטאר די פֿואירה ·

108   קי דילאנטירו קישֿיירה ·   קי פשאשֿין די יוסף.׃

רצד   עשו דישטה מנירה ·   לואיגו אובו פֿבלאדו ·

59]   אישטה קואיבה מיאה אירה ·   קי יו לה אובֿי איריֿדאדו ·

קי מי פֿדרי מי לה דיירה ·   קי יו שו מיוראדו ·

112   אי לואיגו רישפונדיירה ·   אשו טיאו יוסף.׃

[רצה] אק(וא)ישטה קואיבה אירה ·   די אברם איל אונרדו ·

אי דישפואיש איל לה דיירה ·   אה יצחק איל שו נאדו ·

105. פִֿיזְיֵירה] The vowel points are in the same ink as the consonants. פדרי] The י is written as two dots close together. Comp. ll. 14, 18, 26.

106. Between אי and אירה, אינדי was first written and subsequently struck out by the scribe. לי] The י is linked up with the ending of the ל, so that it has the appearance of a ו. פֿואירה] It would seem that the ו has been pointed with a šureq, but this is not certain. A short and very fine dash over the same letter is surely meaningless.

107. פִֿיזיירה] The diacritic mark is very faint. אישטאר] A dash over the ר strikes out two dots šᵉwa-like under the א of פֿואירה in the preceding line.

108. די] It ends the line in the MS. קישֿיירה] The third י is almost confused with the turning of the ר, but it is certain.

109. אובו] Possibly the diacritic mark on the ב is confused with the ending of the ן of פשאשֿין in the preceding line.

110. איריֿדאדו] A dot, surely meaningless, appears above the first י.

111. יֿו] The dot is on the י, but it seems to represent a holem.

113. אק(וא)ישטה] The scribe first wrote אי אישטה. Then ק was written over the first י. ו was due to attraction by the following קואי-.

24

[293]   Yoçef todo lo fizyeraʰ   Komo el padre dixeraʰ.
     'Esaw, su ermano i eraʰ,   Kontralyador le fueraʰ.
     Laʰ ǧente el fizyeraʰ   Todaʰ estar de fueraʰ,
     Ke delantero kisieraʰ   Ke pasasen de Yoçef.   108

294   'Esaw destaʰ maneraʰ   Luego obo fablado:
     "Estaʰ kuebaʰ miaʰ eraʰ,   Ke yo laʰ ove eredado:
     Ke mi padre me laʰ dieraʰ,   Ke yo so mayorado".
     E luego respondieraʰ   Asu tio Yoçef: 112

[295]   "Akestaʰ kuebaʰ eraʰ   De Abram, el onrado,
     E despues el laʰ dieraʰ   Aʰ Yiṣḥaq, el su nado.

[293] Joseph faithfully fulfilled his father's charge, but Esau thereto was opposed. He caused the people to stay without [the cave], for he wished that Joseph should pass out thence before [them].

294 Then spake Esau in this wise unto him: "The cave was mine, for [truly] I did inherit it. My father gave it to me as I am his first-born". Then answered Joseph unto his uncle:

[295] "The cave verily did belong unto Abraham, the honoured one,

105. The metre requires the apocope of the final -o in *todo*: *Yoçef tod(o) lo fizyeraʰ*. See MPidal *Cantar* II, § 45, 3. A similar apocope should be effected in the second half lines: *Kom(o) el padre dizeraʰ* (comp. *kom* 3, 88, 147).

106. *'Esaw, su ermano i eraʰ*: The scribe wrote *'Esaw, su ermano i ende*, and after having struck out *ende*, he added *eraʰ*. The substitution seems due to the desire of uniforming the internal rime. The original reading might well have been as the scribe first wrote. This is assumed in the translation.   *kontralyador* 'opponent'. It is the שׂטן in Yashar (see p. 44).

107. *de fueraʰ*: See MPidal *Cantar* II, § 179, 4.

108. *pasasen de*: Read *pasas ende* or *pasas[e] ende*. But *de* may be a scribal addition.

110. *ke yo*: The metre favours the suppression of *ke* here and at the beginning of the ensuing line.

114. *nado*: A past participle used as a noun. On the more current use of this word in its original function, see Apol II, s.v. *naçer*; as a pronoun or indefinite adjective, MPidal *Cantar* II, § 76, 2.

די יצחק לה אובײרה ٠ מי פדרי אירידאדו ٠

אי לואינו רישפונדײרה ٠ עשו איושׁף ٠.٠   116

[רצו] שׁי ווש אוטרוש שבידיש ٠ די אקישטה אירידאת ٠

טאליש קרטאש מושטרידיש ٠ ורידיש שׁי איש וירדאת ٠

אי לואינו לו פרובארידיש ٠ שיאה אשׁי אווש בונדאת ٠

שובֿרי אישטו נון פֿבלידיש ٠ ווש אוטרוש נין יושׁף ٠.٠   120

[רצו] אה נפתלי דישׁירה ٠ יושׁף איל שׁו אירמנו ٠   [59ש]

אנדה וֵי טו קארירה ٠ אה אאיבטו די מאנו ٠

טראימי אה אישׁטה טיירה ٠ קרטאש די אישקריבאנו ٠

אי נפתלי פֿיזײרה ٠ קומו מאנדו יושׁף ٠.٠   124

115. The dot at the end of the first half line is uncertain.

119. [אשׁי] The י is merely a dot. Two very faint dots are discernible in the rotograph in the space underneath the line between this י and the א of אווש. Their position precludes us from taking them as a ṣere attached to the י.

121. [דישׁירה] The rotograph shows a meaningless dot under the שׁ.

De Yiṣḥaq la^h obiera^h Mi padre eredado".
E luego respondiera^h 'Esaw aYoçef: 116

[296] "Si vos otros sabedes   De akesta^h eredath,
Tales kartas mostredes,   Veredes si es verdath.
E luego lo probaredes.   Sia^h asi avos bondath,
Sobre esto non fabledes   Vos otros nin Yoçef". 120

[297] A^h Naftali dixera^h Yoçef, el su ermano:
"Anda^h, ve tu karera^h A^h Aibto de mano;
Trayeme a^h esta^h tiera^h Kartas de eskribano".
E Naftali fizyera^h Komo mando Yoçef.   124

who in aftertime did give it unto his son Isaac. From Isaac my father inherited it". And then Esau to Joseph thus answered:

[296] "If aught concerning this inheritance ye know, ye should bring forth such writings that the truth may be made known to you. Then ye may prove it [your case?]. If there be goodness in you(?) of this neither ye nor Joseph should speak".

[297] Joseph to his brother Naftali said: "Make haste and straightway get thee into Egypt and bring hither to me the writings of the men of law". And Naftali did as he was commanded by Joseph.

117. *sabedes de*: Comp. Apol 125b; DL no. 64, 14.

118. *tales*: See MPidal *Cantar* p. 336, 17 on the omission of the correlative *que*. In the ending of *veredes* there is perhaps an error due to attraction by the preceding *-edes*. The first person plural was possibly intended.

119. *sia^h asi avos bondath*: A difficult passage: *asi* seems to be a dittography. Possibly this half line should replace 118b. Alternatively ll. 118–20 may mean: "such deeds ye should bring forth that we may know the truth. Then ye shall prove your case, if there is goodness in you. Neither ye...etc."

122. *karera^h*: See MPidal *Cantar* III, s.v. JRuiz 1524c, etc. דרך is thus translated in BFerrar and PConst. *de mano* 'directly'. Usual.

123. *trayeme*: Read *trayem(e)*. Comp. *entregom* Shem Tob*C* fol. 30*v*. On the 'iotización' see MPidal *Cantar* II, §§ 28; 82, 1; RArch vi, 278.

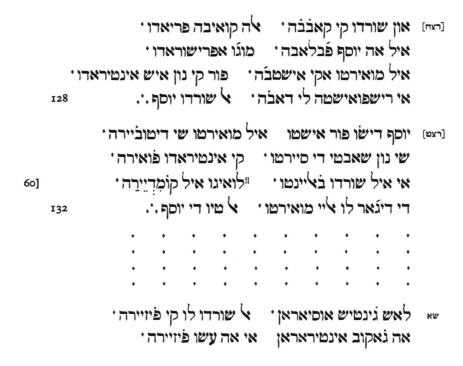

[רצח] און שֿורדו קי קאבֿבֿה ׃   אה קואיבה פֿריאדו ׃

איל אה יוסף פֿבֿלאבֿה ׃   מוגֿו אפֿרישׁוראדו ׃

איל מוארטו אקי אישׁטבֿה ׃   פֿור קי נון איש אינטיראדו ׃

אי רישׁפֿואישׁטה לי דאבֿה ׃   אֿ שֿורדו יוסף ׃׃   128

[רצט] יוסף דישֿו פֿור אישׁטו   איל מוארטו שֿי דיטובֿיירה ׃

שֿי נון שׁאבֿטי די סיירטו ׃   קי אינטיראדו פֿואירה ׃

אי איל שֿורדו באֿינטו ׃   "לואיגו איל קֿומֿדְיֵירַה ׃   60]

די דינֿאר לו אֿיי מוארטו ׃   אֿ טיו די יוסף ׃׃   132

   ׃   ׃   ׃   ׃   ׃   ׃   ׃   ׃   ׃   ׃

   ׃   ׃   ׃   ׃   ׃   ׃   ׃   ׃   ׃   ׃

   ׃   ׃   ׃   ׃   ׃   ׃   ׃   ׃   ׃   ׃

   ׃   ׃   ׃   ׃   ׃   ׃   ׃   ׃   ׃   ׃

שׁא לאשׁ גֿינטישׁ אוסיאראן ׃   אֿ שֿורדו לו קי פֿיזֿיירה ׃

אה גֿאקוב אינטיריאראן ׃   אי אה עשֿו פֿיזֿיירה ׃

132. Underneath this line the Hebrew words חסר אחת 'one [stanza] is missing' appear. Between this note, which is in the scribe's hand, and the following stanza there is a blank of six lines. These are indicated by dots on the left of the page, corresponding to the beginning of a line. This blank, as that on fol. 60 *v*, may correspond to others in the MS. from which the present one is a copy. Or else the scribe was unable to transcribe the missing stanzas, owing, perhaps, to the bad state of preservation of the text before him.

[298]   Un sordo ke kavavaʰ   Alaʰ kuebaʰ priado,
       El aʰ Yoçef fablabaʰ   Muǧo apresurado:
       "El muerto aki estavaʰ: Por ke non es enterado?"
       E respuestaʰ le davaʰ   Al sordo Yoçef.   128

[299]   Yoçef dixo: "Por esto   El muerto se detuvieraʰ;
       Si non, sabte de çierto   Ke enterado fueraʰ".
       E el sordo valiento   Luego el komidyeraʰ
       De deǧar lo alyi muerto   Al tio de Yoçef.   132

       · · · · · · · · · ·
       · · · · · · · · · ·
       · · · · · · · · · ·
       · · · · · · · · · ·

301   Las ǧentes oçiaran   Al sordo lo ke fizyeraʰ.
       Aʰ Ǧakob enteraran   E [i] 'Esaw fizyeraʰ

[298] A deaf man was digging diligently in the cave. Forthwith to Joseph he spake in haste: "The body lieth here, why is it not buried?" And Joseph answered unto the deaf man,

[299] Saying, "For this cause the burial was hindered, for otherwise be thou sure that verily the body would have been buried". Then the valiant deaf one purposed in his heart thereupon to kill Joseph's uncle.

301 · · · · · · · · · All praised the deaf man for the deed that he had done. Then was Jacob buried. And Esau besieged [Joseph's followers] where they had

129. Read *el muerto s(e) detuvieraʰ*.

130. *sabte*: Comp. "ke sab ke non naçieste" Shem Tob*C* fol. 23 ("que sabe..." *E* fol. 39).

131. *valiento*: The ending -*o* has possibly been introduced in order to obtain the assonance. But this form would be possible in Aragonese, a feature of which dialect is to give inflexional endings to adjectives that phonologically should be invariable for gender: comp. *covardo* Alex*O* 124; *tristo* Yuçuf*B* 206; *grando* ibid. *A* 62 b (RArch vi, 282); Shem Tob*C*, passim.

133. *las ǧentes*: 'everybody'. As MCid 3641 (MPidal *Cantar* p. 388, 13). *oçiaran*: *oçiar* 'to praise', as the context shows. Comp. OFr *alcier* 'mettre en honneur' Godefroy s.v.

134. *i*: The MS. has *aʰ*. Clearly a scribal error.

סירקה דו לו אינטיראראן ׃ יוסף לו אנדודייר׳ה ׃

[שב] 136   אה אאיבטו ויניראן ׃ טודוש קון יוסף ׃׃׃

[שב] אה אאיבטו שי טורנארן ׃ אקישה גודיריאה ׃

60v] אילוש שי אפריטמארן ׃ לואיגו אינישי דיאה ׃

אי אין יוסף פינשארן ׃ קי ליש פ̇ארי פ̇וליאה ׃

140   פור קי אילוש איג̇אראן ׃ אין פ̇וזו אה יוסף ׃׃׃

        ׃   ׃   ׃   ׃   ׃   ׃   ׃   ׃   ׃

        ׃   ׃   ׃   ׃   ׃   ׃   ׃   ׃   ׃

        ׃   ׃   ׃   ׃   ׃   ׃   ׃   ׃   ׃

        ׃   ׃   ׃   ׃   ׃   ׃   ׃   ׃   ׃

[שד] לואגו אה יוסף לינארון ׃ אל פלאסיו דו אירה ׃

אי לואיגו שי אינ̇ארון ׃ דילנטי דיל אין טיירה ׃

135. אנדודייר׳ה] The second ד is clear in the MS.

139. פ̇וליאה] The omission of a י after the ל to denote the palatal *ll* is possibly an oversight. Comp. לינארון 141.

140. פור קי] The י is blurred. אין] There is a meaningless dot close to the top right of the א. A blank of three lines (with room for a complete stanza) occurs between this stanza and the following. In this space another hand has written טב טנטו, and just above the beginning of stanza 304, lines 138–9 have been copied. This hand has then copied the rest of the present stanza and the beginning of the next one on the right margin and at the bottom of the page. This scribe uses a horizontal dash over the ג of אינ̇ארן, as a diacritic mark.

141. אל] A dash occurs under this word, which does not seem intended, however, for a *pathaḥ*.

Çerka^h do lo enteraran: Yoçef lo andu[r]iera^h.
A^h Aibto vinieran   Todos kon Yoçef.   136

[302] A^h Aibto se tornaran   Akesa^h ǧuderia^h.
Elyos se apretaran   Luego enese dia^h,
E en Yoçef pensaran   Ke les farie folia^h,
Por ke elyos eǧaran   En pozo a^h Yoçef.   140

·   ·   ·   ·   ·   ·   ·   ·   ·
·   ·   ·   ·   ·   ·   ·   ·   ·
·   ·   ·   ·   ·   ·   ·   ·   ·
·   ·   ·   ·   ·   ·   ·   ·   ·

[304] Luego a^h Yoçef legaron,   Al palaçio do era^h,
E luego se eǧaron   Delante del en tiera^h,

buried him. But Joseph withstood him. All came back to Egypt with Joseph.

[302] Those Jews returned then to Egypt. Then they became anxious lest they should fall under the wrath of Joseph, because aforetime they had cast him into the pit.

·   ·   ·   ·   ·   ·   ·

[304] Then to Joseph they came, unto the mansion where he was. And

135. e [i] 'Esaw fiziera^h çerka^h: Emend e [i] 'Esaw in accordance with Yashar (see p. 46). 'Esaw is a collective. fazer çerka^h 'to besiege'. The first lo refers to Ǧakob.   lo anduriera^h: The reading andudiera^h in the MS. is obviously erroneous. Comp. endurido AlexO 327b, Apol 439b. Here it apparently stands for 'he overcame them'.

137. Read a^h Aibto s(e) tornaran.

138. se apretaran: 'they became anxious' (?). Comp. "i ši açertaba el kwando se ap^{e}retaba" RAlex fol. 13^v, where apretar 'to grow heated in battle', according to the editor.

139. en Yoçef pensaran ke les farie folia^h: en=end. For the construction, see MPidal Cantar II, p. 201, 8. les farie folia^h 'he would behave in a spirit of revenge towards them'.

141. legaron: llegar 'to come forward', as in MCid 1513.

31

אי טודוש לו אדורארון ·   אין מוי פֿואירטי מנירה ·

144   אי טודוש אי פֿבלארון ·   לואיגו קון יוסף ·׃

[שח]   דיזיין נון פֿאריש מייניטיש ·   יוסף נואישטרוש ״פֿיקאדוש ·   [61]

שיאירטימוש שירויינטיש ·   אי נוש שומוש קולפֿאדוש ·

אי אוטרושי שירויינטיש ·   קום לוש אינפֿירוגֿאדרוש ·

148   פֿארימוש טוש טאלינטיש ·   פֿורה שיימפֿרי יוסף ·׃

[שי]   יוסף קואנדו לו אואירה ·   ליוראבֿה די לוש אוגֿוש ·

אי לואיגו לוש דישירה ·   אֵקֵי טומאדיש קירדוגֿוש ·

קי אין אקישטה טיירה ·   נון אברידיש אינוגֿוש ·

152   קי יא מירסיד אובֿיירה ·   די איליוש יוסף ·׃

144. פֿבלארון] The diacritic is close to the falling stroke of the ן of אדורארון in the preceding line.

145. פֿיקאדוש [יוסף נואישטרוש] Possibly by another hand. Three dots arranged in a triangle appear above the -פֿי.

146. The point denoting the end of the line is very faint, but unmistakable.

149. אואירה] A dot, clearly a later addition, appears between the and the ר.

32

E todos lo adoraron   En mui fuerte manera^h,

E todos i fablaron   Luego kon Yoçef,   144

[305]   Dizien: "Non pares mientes,   Yoçef, nuestros
pekados:

Seertemos servientes.   E nos, somos kulpados;

E otrosi servientes   Kom los enferoğados,

Faremos tus talentes   Pora^h siempre, Yoçef".   148

[306]   Yoçef kuando lo oy[e]ra^h,   Lyorava^h de los oğos;

E luego los dixera^h: "Ake tomades kordoğos?

Ke en akesta^h tiera^h   Non abredes enoğos";

Ke ya merçed obiera^h   De elyos Yoçef.   152

they fell down before him to the earth, and they all implored him earnestly. And thus they all spake to Joseph,

[305] Saying: "O Joseph, look not upon our transgressions; we shall be thy bondsmen; behold our trespasses we confess unto thee. And serving thee as bondmen thy will we shall do for ever, O Joseph!"

[306] When Joseph heard this he wept exceedingly. Then he said unto them: "Why are ye distressed? In this land shall ye not be troubled". For Joseph now had compassion on them.

---

145. *dizien*: Probably a participle or gerund, as in Yuçuf*A* 42 c (see RArch vi, 278). *non pares mientes...nuestros pekados*: Comp. "e los sabios entienden esto; que paran mientes sus postrimerias" Grünbaum p. 97.

146. *e nos*: *e* is the demonstrative adverb, which Romance orthography spells *fe, he*. In the present instance it corresponds to Hebr. הגנו (Gen 50, 18), which PConst renders by *hek*: "hek nos ati por sierbos" (fol. 98*v*).

148. *pora^h*: Also in Shem Tob*C*, along with *para^h*. It is preserved in the fourteenth-century MSS. of *Apolonio*, and *Buenos Proverbios*, and in Aragon it lingers in early fifteenth-century documents (see *Docum. Hist. Aragón* iv, p. 510, and passim).

149. *kuando lo oy[e]ra^h*: In view of the prevalence of hiatus in our poem, even between identical vowels, apocopation of *-o* in *kuando* is likely. The text has *oira^h*. But omission of a ʾ is, in view of the rime, quite likely. On this form, see Staaff p. 295; Gassner p. 183. *lyorava^h de los oğos*: See MPidal *Cantar* pp. 92, 736; Apol ii, s.v.

150. *los dixera^h*: It is not a case of 'loísmo' in the dative (see MPidal *Cantar* ii, § 130, 2). *kordoğos*: Comp. SDom 340, JRuiz 61 d, etc.

שז   יוסף לואיגו פֿבלאבֿה ·   אקישאש רזוניש ·

אי בֿיין לוש אנאבבֿה ·   אה אקישוש וארוניש ·

אי לואיגו שושינגאבֿה ·   איל לוש שוש קוראסוניש ·

156   קי מוי בֿיין לוש אמאבֿה ·   אטודוש יוסף ּ׃·

[שח]   יוסף לוש מאנטו[בֿ]יירה ·   אי נון קון שוֹנְשאנְיוֹש ·

[61 ע]   אי איל בֿיין קישטו פֿואירה ·   די שויש אי די אישטראניוש ·

אי פור קואינטה ביבֿיירה ·   סינטו אי דייז אניוש ·

160   אינאנטיש קי מורײרה   פֿיזו טישטאמינטו יוסף ּ׃·

[שט]   דיונדי ײאזײ אי דוליינטי ·   יוסף אובו פֿבלאדו ·

דישׂירה אה מוא[י]רטי ·   די ווש וֹ מאנזיליײאדו ·

קאטיבֿירױ מוי פֿואירטי ·   ווש אברידי[ש] ...וֹ ·

164   אין טודה אקישטה גינטי ·   שא...[ה] פור יו[ס]ֿפֿ ּ׃·

---

157. מאנטובֿיירה] The diacritic point over the בֿ is very faint.

158. אי איל] are faint. קישטו] The top left of the ט is very blurred. פֿואירה] The upper part of the ו is blurred. אניוש-] The top of the ו and the י are blurred.

159. The dot marking the end of the half line is doubtful.

161. דיונדי] דונדי was first written before, and subsequently struck out. The present reading immediately follows the word struck out. Although the writing is in both slightly larger than usual, the hand is undoubtedly the same as the rest of the MS.

162. מוארטי] The first י is very faint, but unmistakable.

163. קאטיבֿירױ] The top of the בֿ is blurred. [ש]אברידי] The beginning and the falling stroke of the ש are visible. This is followed by the upper turning of a possible פ. But the rest of this word, with the exception of a final ו, is illegible.

164. שא...ה] This is followed by a possible ו. Another of the missing letters might be a ד or ר. The left and horizontal strokes of the final ה are faintly visible. יוסף] The ס is blurred.

34

307   Yoçef luego fablava^h   Akesas razones,
E bien los agabava^h   A^h akesos varones,
E luego sosegava^h   El los sus koraçones:
Ke mui bien los amava^h   Atodos Yoçef.   156

[308]   Yoçef los mantuviera^h   E non kon sonsanyos.
E el bien kisto fuera^h   De suyos e de estranyos.
E por kuenta^h bibiera^h   Çiento e diez anyos.
Enantes ke muriera^h   Fizo testamento Yoçef.   160

[309]   Deonde yazie i(?) doliente,   Yoçef ovo fablado;
Dixera^h ala^h muerte: "De vos vo manzilyado:
Katiberio mui fuerte   Vos abredes . . . [ad]o
En toda^h akesta^h ǧente   Sal[vada?]^h por Yoçef".   164

307 Joseph then spake these words, and right well those men he praised, and their hearts he set at rest, for well did Joseph love them all.

[308] Joseph cared for them, and with no mockery [i.e. in no trifling manner], whilst well loved was he alike by strangers and kinsmen. He lived by true reckoning a hundred and ten years. Before his death Joseph made his will.

[309] Whilst he was lying sick Joseph spake. At the time of death he said: "For ye I feel compassion: a sore captivity shall ye endure(?) amidst all this people whom Joseph saved".

154. *agabava*^h: *agabar* 'to praise', comp. Alex*P* 13d (*gabar* ibid. 52, 119, etc.); see Ro iv, 45. Also BProv fol. 63 (Knust Mittheil p. 22), RAlex fol. 93.

157. *sonsanyos*: Comp. Shem Tob*E* fol. 82: "Lo que ami en plaze[r] viene Otro ha por sonsaño [agravio *C*]". Also Elena 8. Comp. *sosaños* MCid 1020, Apol ii, s.v., etc.

159. *por kuenta*^h: 'precisely, by exact reckoning' (MPidal *Cantar* iii, s.v.).

160. *enantes ke muriera*^h: Comp. MCid 302, VTristan 129, 21.   *fizo testamento Yoçef*: This being the only sure octosyllable in our fragment, apocopation in *testamento* is likely (see MPidal *Cantar* ii, § 40; Apol ii, 7; RHi lxxvii, 455).

162. *ala*^h *muerte*: See MPidal *Cantar* ii, § 183, 3.   *vo manzilyado*: Possibly an error of transcription, for *so manzilyado*.

דיז טודוש אישטארידיש ׳   אין א[א]יב[טו קאטיבוש ׳

אי דישפואיש ווש שירידיש ׳   חורוש אי נון קא[ט]יבוש ׳

אי די אקי שאלדי(י)רידיש ׳   טודוש שאנוש אי ביבוש ׳

קון וושקו ליבארידיש ׳   לוש אואישוש די יוסף .׳.

168

165. [איבטו]   -איב- are blurred.

166. [קאטיבוש]   The top of the ק is blotted, and the ט is blurred.

167. [שאלדירידיש]   There are two dots under the ל. These may be taken for a vowel point, which would be meant for the following ר. This letter partly falls within the lower stroke of the ל. The scribe seems to have first written -שאלייר, and then added the ר after the ל, forgetting to cancel one of the two יי.

168. [יוסף]   The top of the ס is blurred.

36

[310]   Diz: "Todos estaredes   En Aibto katibos,
      E despues vos seredes   Ḥoros e non kativos,
      E de aki salderedes   Todos sanos e bivos.
      Kon vusko lebaredes   Los uesos de Yoçef".   168

[310] He said: "Ye shall remain captive in Egypt, but later ye shall be free and not captives. Ye shall come out herefrom all alive and hale. Ye shall carry with you Joseph's bones".

167. *salderedes*: For the details of epenthetic vowels in Spanish, see MPidal *Or* § 40. In late medieval MSS. Pietsch considers this feature an indication of Leonese origin (see MPhil xiii, 642). Comp. *saldera* JRuiz*T* 1332. It is not rare in Shem Tob*C*: *tereverie* 15*v* (*treveria* M), *kereçer* 39 (*cresçer* M), *balderiemos* 46*v* (*valdremos* E). Such epentheses are also characteristic of the Morisco speech (RArch vi, 113).

PARALLELS AND SOURCES

THE fragment begins with the vision of Jacob at Beer-Sheba. Stanza 260 probably coincided with Gen 46, 1. "E dixo el señor a Jacob, que es Israel, en la revelaçion de la noche. Dixole: Jacob. Jacob dixo: Heme. E dixo: Yo so el Dios de tu padre. Non temas de ir a Egipto, que generaçion te fare ende. Yo desçendere contigo a Egipto, e yo te alçare dende e sobire. E Joseph te ponera la mano sobre tus ojos" BAlba p. 87.

4. Possibly *E [ve] tomar talentes*, in accordance with Yashar (p. 183): Jacob wishes to know if the fear of his God is still in Joseph's heart:

אל תירא מיוסף כי עודנו מחזיק בתומתו לעבדני כאשר ייטב
בעיניך וישמח יעקב מאד מאד על בנו

"[And the Lord said unto Jacob], Fear not about Joseph, for he still retaineth his integrity to serve Me, as it will be seen good in thy sight. And Jacob rejoiced exceedingly concerning his son".

10. Gen. 46, 5. In the usual *Midrashim*, no reference is found to the material of which the chariots were made.

11–12. Gen 46, 28. Comp. Josephus, *Ant. Iud.* 2, 7, 5.

13. "Et ensillo Josep su cavalgadura e salio a resçebir a Israel, su padre, a tierra de Gosen. E commo le vido echose sobre sus çervizes, e lloro sobre sus çervizes mas. E dixo Israel a Josepe: Agora yo muriese, despues que vi las tus fazes; que eras aun bivo" BEsc p. 64b (Gen 46, 29–30).

15. This incident is not midrasic. Yashar (p. 184) merely says: ויחבק גם יוסף את אביו וישקהו "And Joseph also embraced his father and kissed him".

18. *vistu e alegria*[h]: This comes from Yashar, ibid. ויאמר יעקב אל יוסף הנה אמותה הפעם בטובה אחרי אשר ראיתי את פניך "And Jacob said unto Joseph, Now I will die cheerfully after I have seen thy face".

21. Gen. 46, 31–4. "Et dixo Josep a sus ermanos e a los de la casa de su padre: Sobire e contare a Faraon, a dezir le he: Mis ermanos e los

39

de la casa de mi padre, que estavan en tierra de Canaan, me vinieron. E los omnes son pastores de ganados. E sus ovejas e sus vacas e todo lo suyo troxieron. E sera quando vos llamase Faraon e vos dixere: Que son las vuestras obras? E diredes: Omnes de ganado fueron tus siervos desde nuestra moçedat fasta agora, tanbien nosotros commo nuestros anteçessores" BEsc ibid.

23. *la çibdath*: The Ἡρώων πόλις of Ios. *Ant. l.c.* Comp. "Mas dize maestre Pedro...que estos dos logares Jersen e Ramesse que en una tierra son, e aun que aquella tierra, pero que ouo dantes nombre Jersen, que essa es ala que despues, e aun dantes, llamaron Thebas, dond fueron los reyes Thebeos...e diz aun como poblaron otrossi estonces estos reyes una uilla en aquella tierra dond eran naturales, e llamaron la por nombre la Cibdad delos Sennores....E a esta cibdath que dizien delos Sennores salio Josep a recebir assu padre, segund cuenta Josepho" GEst p. 239. See P.Comestor, *Historia Scholastica*, cap. 98 (Migne, *Patr. Lat.*, vol. 198, col. 1134).

The contents of the missing stanzas were probably based on Gen 47, 1–12. "E veno Josep e conto a Faraon, e dixole: Mi padre e mis ermanos, e sus ovejas e sus vacas e todo lo suyo vinieron de tierra de Canaan. E helos en tierra de Gosen. Et de parte de sus ermanos tomo çinco omnes e parolos ante Faraon. Et dixo Faraon a sus ermanos: Que son las vuestras obras? Et dixeron a Faraon: Pastores de ganados son tus siervos, tanbien commo nuestros anteçessores. E dixeron: Para en la tierra venimos; que non han pasto las ovejas de tus siervos, que es muy grande la fanbre en tierra de Canaan. E agora esten tus siervos en tierra de Gosen. Et dixo Faraon a Josep: Tu padre e tus ermanos son venidos a ty. La tierra de Egipto ante ty es. En lo mejor de la tierra faz estar a tu padre e a tus ermanos. Moren en tierra de Gosen. E si sabes que ay en ellos algunos omnes de fuerça, e ponerlos has de mayorales de ganado sobre todo lo mio. Et metio Josep a Jacob, su padre, a fizolo estar ante Faraon. E bendixo Jacob a Faraon. Et dixo Faraon a Jacob: Quantos son los dias de tus annos de tus vidas? Et dixo Jacob a Faraon: Los dias de annos de mis moradas son çiento e treynta annos; pocos e malos fueron los annos de mis vidas, e non alcançaron a los dias de annos de mis anteçesores en dias de sus moradas. Et bendixo Jacob a Faraon e salio de ante Faraon. E fizo morar Josep a su padre e a sus ermanos; e dioles heredat en tierra de Egipto en lo mejor de la tierra, en tierra de Ramaçes, commo mando Faraon" BEsc p. 65.

29. Gen 47, 13–15 "E pan non avia en toda la tierra, que era muy fuerte la fanbre. E peresçia tierra de Egipto e tierra de Canaan por la fanbre. E apanno Josep toda la plata que fue fallada en tierra de Egipto e en tierra de Canaan por el pan que ellos conpravan, e troxo Josep la plata a casa de Faraon. Et atemose la plata en tierra de Egipto e en tierra de Canaan, e vinieron los Egipçianos a Josep diziendo: E por que morremos ante ty, pues se acabo la plata?" BEsc ibid.

32. Gen 47, 16–17. "Dixoles Joseph: Datme vuestros ganados, ca yo vos dare pan por vuestros ganados, pues dezides que es ya atamada la plata. E troxieron sus ganados a Joseph. E dioles Joseph pan por los cavallos e por el ganado ovejuno e vacuno e por los asnos. E mantovolos de pan en aquel año por sus ganados" BAlba p. 89.

35. *la ǧente dese[s]ada*[h]: Gen 47, 13, where ותלה ארץ מצרים is rendered "e andavan desvariados los de la tierra de Egipto" in BAlba p. 89, and "i enlokeçiose tiera de Miṣrayim" in PConst fol. 91a, l. 5 below.

37. Gen 47, 18–19. "Et acabose ese anno. E venieron en el anno segundo e dixeronle: Non negaremos de mi sennor que se nos atamo la plata, e el ganado de la quatropea es de mi sennor. Non queda ante mi sennor salvo nuestros cuerpos e nuestras tierras: por que morremos a tu ojo? Tan bien nos commo nuestras tierras tuyos seremos. Conpra a nos e a nuestras tierras por el pan, e seremos nos e nuestras tierras siervos de Faraon. E danos symiente e bivamos e non muramos, e la tierra non se desolara" BEsc p. 65.

45. Gen 47, 23–4. "Y dixo Yoseph al pueblo: He compre a vos oy y a vuestra tierra a Parho: he a vos simiente y sembraredes a la tierra. Y sera en los renuevos: Y daredes quinto a Parho, y quatro las partes sera para vos, para simiente del campo y para vuestro comer y para los que en vuestras casas, y para comer para vuestras familia. Y dixeron: Abiviguaste nos. Fallemos graçia en ojos de mi señor, y seremos siervos a Parho" BFerrar fols. 23d–24a.

53. Gen 47, 22, 26. "De çierto tiera[h] de los monagos non kompro, ke fuero a[h] los monagos de kon Par'o. I komian asu fuero ke dio aelyos Par'o: por tanto non vendieron asu tiera[h]" PConst fol. 92a. The other biblical versions have 'saçerdotes' for כהנים. BAlba (p. 89) says 'saçerdotes e ministros' in v. 22, and 'clerigos' in v. 26. Comp. "Cuenta la estoria que libres fincaron de seer vendudos e siervos, la

41

tierra e heredamientos delos saçerdotes e los saçerdotes mismos....E
demas diz la estoria que les davan delos çilleros de Pharaon alos saçerdotes cosa estaiada pora sus espensas. Et el rey et Josep, quelo avie de
veer por mandado del rey, non les quisieron por tod aquello menguar
nada delo que avien a aver, mas mantovieron los en su fecho; e esto era
otra razon que por ende non ovieron ninguna premia por que vendiesen
nin enagenasen sus heredades, nin las vendieron" GEst p. 243a.

57. *Yoçef*: In view of Targum Ionathan (Gen 50, 3), which states
that the famine in Egypt came to an end after two years because of the
merits of Jacob, we may suspect an error of transmission here, and read
Ğakob instead of *Yoçef*. As far as I have been able to ascertain there is
no tradition in Rabbinic literature attributing the suspension of the
visitation to Joseph's prayers.

61. Gen 45, 18.

62. Gen 47, 28.

63. To Gen 47, 11, Yashar adds (p. 184) that "the sons of Jacob ate
the best of the whole land: the best of Egypt all the days of Joseph".

64. Gen 47, 29–31. "E acercaronse los dias de Israel para morir, e
llamo a su fijo Josep e dixole: Si agora alcançe graçia en tus ojos, pon tu
mano so mi anca. E faras comigo merçed e verdad, que non me sotierres
en Egipto. Yazere con mis anteçesores. E levarme as de Egipto, e
soterrarme as en sus fonsarios. E dixole: Yo fare tu mandado. Et
dixole: Jurame. E jurole" BEsc p. 66.

73. Gen 49, 1–27.

76. Gen 48, 22; 49, 22–26.

77. Gen 49, 33.

82. *fizo vanyar al muerto*: Comp. "Mos enim erat ethnicorum in-
condita servare corpora novem diebus, et singulis diebus plangere, et
fovere ea calida aqua, ut sciretur utrum anima egressa an sopita foret;
condita vero undecim servabant" P.Comestor, *op. cit*. cap. 114 (Migne,
loc. cit. col. 1140). Comestor relies in this point on Rabbinic tradition.
See P.Perdrizet, *Le Speculum Humanae Salvationis* (Paris 1908), pp. 89–90.
"Quando Josep vio finado asu padre, con el grand pesar e el grand
dolor que ovo dend, corrio e dexos caer sobrel, e començo a besar le,
maguer que era ya finado, e llorar mucho e fazer grande duelo por
el....Desi mando asus fijos, que eran y conel, quel balsamassen. Et
ellos vannaron le muy bien e desi balsamaron le" GEst p. 256b.

83. Jacob's bier was covered with a cloth of gold, according to the tradition incorporated in Yashar (p. 188, 27).

86. According to the Yashar version, *l.c.*, "all the people of Egypt, and the elders and all the inhabitants of the land of Goshen wept and mourned over Jacob, and all his sons and the children of his household lamented and mourned over their father Jacob". Comp. Gen 50, 3.

87. Comp. Rashi on Gen 50, 3. P.Comestor, *Historia Scholastica* 114 (Migne, *Patrol. Lat.* 198, col. 1140). "E Josep, por fazer asu padre mayor onra que a otro omne fuera fecha en aquel logar fasta aquella sazon, quiso que amas aquellas costumbres, delos gentiles et delos judios, se cumpliessen en su padre Jacob asu muerte. E segund esto fue guardado Jacob por soterrar lxx dias, los xxx delos judios e los quarenta delos gentiles" GEst p. 256b.

89. Gen 50, 4–6. As in Yashar (p. 188, 15), however, Joseph does not speak to the household of the Pharaoh, but to the Pharaoh himself.

97. Gen 50, 7–10. "Y subio Yoseph a enterrar a su padre. Y subieron con el todos los siervos de Parhoh, viejos de su casa y todos viejos de tierra de Egypto. Y toda casa de Yoseph y sus hermanos y casa de su padre....Y subio con el tambien quatregua, tambien cavalleros. Y fue el real grave mucho. Y vinieron fasta Era de Atad, que allende del Yerden, y oynaron ahi oyna grande y grave mucho. Y hizo a su padre lemuño siete dias" BFerrar fol. 25.

ויוסף וביתו חולכים יחד קרוב אל המטה יחפים ובוכים...... וחמשים מעבדי יעקב הולכים אל פני המטה ויפזרו בכל הדרך מור ואהלות וכל בושם: וכל בני יעקב נושאי המטה הולכים על הבושם: ועבדי יעקב ילכו לפניהם הלוך והשלך כל הבושם על הדרך

"And Joseph and his household were together near the bier barefooted and weeping....And fifty of Jacob's servants went in front of the bier and they strewed along the road myrrh and aloes and all manner of perfume. And all the sons of Jacob that carried the bier walked upon the perfume. And the servants of Jacob went before them strewing the perfume along the road" Yashar p. 189.

101.

וישמעו כל מלכי כנען את הדבר הזה ויצאו איש ממקומו
שלשים ואחד מלכי כנען ויבאו כלם עם כל אנשים לספד ולבכות
את יעקב : ויראו כל המלכים האלה מטת יעקב והנה עליה כתר
יוסף ויקחו גם המה וישימו את כתריהם על המטה ויסובבוה
בכתריהם

"And all the kings of Canaan heard of this thing. And they all went forth
each man from his house thirty-one kings of Canaan, and they all came
with their men to mourn and weep for Jacob. And all these kings beheld
Jacob's bier, and behold Joseph's crown was upon it. And they also
took their crowns and put them upon the bier and encircled it with their
crowns" Yashar ibid. A few lines before (p. 188, 28) it is stated

וישם יוסף על ראש יעקב אביו עטרת זהב גדולה וישם שרביט
הזהב בידו ויסובבו [ויסוככו .v.l] על המטה כמשפט המלכים בחיים

"And Joseph placed upon the head of his father Jacob a large golden
crown, and he put a golden sceptre in his hand. And they surrounded
the bier as was the custom of kings during their lives". Cf. T.B. *Soṭah*.
13a.

106.

ויהי בבואם שם ויעמוד עשו וכל בניו ואנשיו על יוסף ואחיו
לשטן במערה לאמר לא יקבר יעקב בה כי כי לנו ולאבינו היא :
וישמע יוסף ואחיו את דברי בני עשו ויחר אפם מאד ויגש יוסף
אל עשו לאמר : מה הדבר הזה אשר תדברו הלא קנה קנה אותה
יעקב אבי ממך בעושר רב אחרי מות יצחק זה היום עשרים וחמש
שנה...ויען עשו את יוסף לאמר שקר תאמר וכזב תדבר כי לא
מכרתי את אשר לי בכל הארץ הזאת אשר תדבר וגם יעקב אחי
לא קנה מכל אשר לי בארץ הזאת מאומה : ועשו דבר הדברים
האלה למען הכחיש את יוסף בדבריו

"And as they came there Esaw stood with all his sons and his men
against Joseph and his brethren as an opponent in the cave, saying:
Jacob shall not be buried therein, for it belongeth to us and to our fathers.
And Joseph and his brethren heard the words of Esaw's sons, and they
were exceedingly wroth. And Joseph approached Esaw, saying: What

44

is this which you have spoken? Surely my father Jacob bought it from
thee for great riches after the death of Isaac, now five and twenty years
ago....And Esaw answered, saying: Thou speakest falsely and utterest
lies, for I sold not anything belonging to me in all this land, as thou
sayest, neither did my brother Jacob buy aught belonging to me in this
land. And Esaw spoke these things in order to deceive Joseph with his
words" Yashar pp. 189–90. Cf. *Soṭah* ibid.

116.

ויאמר יוסף אל עשו הלא כי ספר המקנה כתב אבי כדברים
האלה עמך ויעד עדים בספר והנו במצרים אתנו: ויען עשו לאמר
לכו הביאנו את הספר ואת כל אשר אמצא בספר ההוא אעשה:
ויקרא יוסף אל נפתלי אחיו ויאמר מהרה חושה אל תעמוד ורוץ
נא מצרימה והבא את כל הספרים את ספר המקנה ואת החתום
ואת הגלוי: וגם כל הספרים הראשונים אשר כתוב בהם את כל
דברי הבכורה קח: והבאת לנו פה ונודע מהם את כל דברי
עשו ובניו אשר ידברו ביום הזה

"And Joseph said unto Esaw, Surely my father inserted these things with
thee in the record of purchase, and testified the record with witnesses,
and behold it is with us in Egypt. And Esaw answered, saying unto him,
Bring me the record, all that I will find in the record, so I will do. And
Joseph called unto Naphtali, his brother, and he said, Hasten quickly,
stay not, and run I pray thee to Egypt and bring all the records; the
record of the purchase, the sealed record and the open record; and also
all the first records in which all the transactions of the birth-right are
written, fetch thou. And thou shalt bring them unto us hither, that we
may know from them all the words of Esaw and his sons which they
spoke this day" Yashar p. 190. Cf. *Soṭah* ibid.

132.

וחושים בן דן בן יעקב היה בעת ההיא את בני יעקב...ישב
עם ילדי בני יעקב על מטת יעקב לשמרה: וחושים היה אלם
מדבר וחרש משמע אך הבין את קול האדם הומה: וישאל לאמר
מדוע לא קברתם המת ומה היא המהומה הגדולה הזאת: ויענוהו
ויגידו לו את דברי עשו ובניו אשר מנעם מלקבר את יעקב
במערה: ויהי בהבינו הדברים אשר עשה עשו ובניו ויחר אפו
מאד עליהם

45

"And Ḥushim, the son of Dan, the son of Jacob, was at that time with Jacob's sons...he remained with the children of Jacob's sons by Jacob's bier to guard it. And Ḥushim was dumb and deaf, still he understood the voice of consternation amongst the men. And he asked, saying (*sic*), Why do you not bury the dead and what is this great consternation? And they answered him the words of Esaw and his sons, who had prevented them from burying Jacob in the cave. And when he understood the things that Esaw and his sons had done, he was exceedingly wroth against them" Yashar ibid. The contents of the missing stanza probably coincided with the subsequent line in Yashar:

וימהר ויקח חרב וירץ אל עשו אל תוך המלחמה ויך את עשו בחרב ויכרות ראשו ממנו וילך למרחוק ויפל עשו מתוך אנשי המלחמה

"And quickly he seized a sword, and he ran to Esaw in the midst of the battle, and he slew Esaw with a sword. And he cut off his head, and it sprang to a distance. And Esaw fell amongst the warriors". Cf. *Soṭah* ibid.

135.

ויהי אחרי כן ויערכו בני עשו מלחמה את בני יעקב, וילחמו בני עשו בבני יעקב בחברון...ותגבר יד יוסף על כל אנשי בני עשו

"And it was after this [after Jacob's burial] that the sons of Esaw waged war with the sons of Jacob. And the sons of Esaw fought with the sons of Jacob in Hebron....And the hand of Joseph prevailed over all the people of the sons of Esaw" Yashar p. 191.

140. Gen 50, 14–15. Comp. Ios. Ant. 2, 8, 1. "Mas temien se del los hermanos quel vernie en miente el fecho que ellos fizieran contra el [i.e. Joseph], e ques querrie vengar dellos desque en su poder los toviesse...e fazer les mal e apremiar los. E fablavan todos dello entre si" GEst p. 260. The subject of the missing stanza was probably that of Gen 50, 16–17: "E encomendaron a Josep diziendo: Tu padre encomendo antes que muriese diziendo: Asy diredes a Josep: Ruegote que perdones agora el yerro de tus ermanos e el su pecado, quete gualardonaron tan mal; e agora perdona el yerro de los fijos de Dios por tu padre. Et lloro Josep quando se lo dixeron" BEsc p. 70. The last phrase corresponds to our l. 149.

46

141–156. Gen 50, 18–21. "E fueron tanbien sus ermanos e echaronse antel e dixeron: Henos por tus siervos. E dixoles Josep: Non temades, ca yo temo a Dios....E agora non temades: Yo vos governare a vos e a vuestras crianças. E conortolos e fablo por su voluntad" BEsc ibid.

159. Gen. 50, 22.

160. Midr. Sekhel Ṭob (Gen 50, 24), ed. Buber, p. 331.

168. Gen 50, 24–25. "E dixo Josep a sus ermanos: Ya yo muero, e Dios se menbrara de vosotros e vos subira desta tierra a la tierra que juro Dios a Abraham e a Ysaque e a Jacob. E aconjuro Josep a los fijos de Ysrael diziendo: Membrarse menbrara Dios de vosotros, e sobiredes mis huesos de aqui" BEsc ibid.

INDEX TO ANNOTATED PASSAGES

onores, koronas de o., 103
onrado, 83

pasarse, 79
pekados, por malos de p., 42
pimentar, 82
pimientaʰ, 85
por, 22
poraʰ, 148
preposition, om. of, 145
priado, 81; privado, 13
proclisis, 6, 7
pronoun: *lo* dat., 99; *los*, 150; en-clitic, 6, 91, 123, 129, 137; pro-clitic, 7

reis, 26

saber de, 117; *sab*, 130
salderedes, 167
segum, 62
serbientes, 50
sonsanyos, 157

talente, fazer buen t., 40; *tomar talentes*, 4
tales, 118
trayeme, 123

-u, 6

valiento, 131
vanyar, 82

Yoçef, 4

INDEX OF POINTED WORDS

For EU product safety concerns, contact us at Calle de José Abascal, 56–1°,
28003 Madrid, Spain or eugpsr@cambridge.org.

www.ingramcontent.com/pod-product-compliance
Ingram Content Group UK Ltd.
Pitfield, Milton Keynes, MK11 3LW, UK
UKHW030902150625
459647UK00021B/2652